Authentic Educating

Robert Leahy

Montante Family Library
D'Youville College

JUL 0 7 2010

UNIVERSITY PRESS OF AMERICA,® INC.
Lanham • Boulder • New York • Toronto • Plymouth, UK

Copyright © 2009 by
University Press of America,® Inc.
4501 Forbes Boulevard
Suite 200
Lanham, Maryland 20706
UPA Acquisitions Department (301) 459-3366

Estover Road
Plymouth PL6 7PY
United Kingdom

All rights reserved
Printed in the United States of America
British Library Cataloging in Publication Information Available

Library of Congress Control Number: 2009925437
ISBN: 978-0-7618-4592-8 (paperback : alk. paper)
eISBN: 978-0-7618-4593-5

Cover photo: Students performing *The Wizard of Oz*.

Mundelein Fenwick Library
D Thruwin College

♾ ™ The paper used in this publication meets the minimum
requirements of American National Standard for Information
Sciences—Permanence of Paper for Printed Library Materials,
ANSI Z39.48—1992

LB
1025.3
.L412
2009

Contents

Foreword

Probably every reader of this book has had the experience of working on some task in school that appeared to be little more than busy work at best, and downright fraudulent learning at worst. Busy work usually involves performing some meaningless task such as memorizing dates or names with no consideration of the significance of these. Such tasks become fraudulent when they are graded as though simply providing correct answers on an exam where subject matter has no meaning to the learner becomes the criterion of high achievement. Unfortunately, too much of school learning and school testing falls into the category of fraudulent learning. In this book, Professor Leahy seeks to show how educating can be truly significant, how it can be *authentic*. Readers will see mirrored in the book many of their own learning experiences that fail to meet the criteria for authenticity, and Leahy provides a wealth of suggestions on how to transform educational events into truly authentic educational events. He also shows the important role that feelings and sharing feelings play in authentic educating.

Drawing on his background in philosophy, Leahy nicely summarizes key philosophical ideas and shows the development of current constructivist thinking. He builds on Gowin's ideas including his Vee heuristic that serves as a tool to understand better what it means to create knowledge. In authentic educating the learner becomes a knowledge creator, invested in seeking the meanings inherent in the materials studied.

Readers will find many of the ideas in this book clearly summarized in concept maps, a knowledge representation tool created in our research program at Cornell University. The reader is invited to build on the maps presented and to construct her/his own concept maps to help take ownership of the ideas presented. Numerous examples from the field of literature are offered to illustrate how to transcend from gathering information to learning from reading to the autonomous creation of personal meanings from readings. Leahy cites Gowin's definition that education changes the meaning of experience, and proceeds to provide guidance to teachers on how to help students take charge of their meaning making and achieving personal growth toward authenticity through authentic educating.

Another helpful feature of Leahy's book is the many examples from his own teaching, including examples of student's work. These are presented along with suggestions as to how your own teaching can encourage authentic educating. This book will be a valuable addition to any teacher's library, and also to the library of any learner who seeks to find genuine significance in learning, a kind of "felt significance" that not only makes learning more successful but also more exciting. For all the education problems we face in the challenging information age we are in, there are no simple solutions. However, Leahy's book helps to point the way we should seek to move if we truly want to prepare our young people not only to be better learners, but also to become citizens that seek to make a positive difference in this competitive, complex world.

Joseph D. Novak
Professor Emeritus, Cornell University

Preface

This book is the product of almost forty years of teaching and writing about education. When I started teaching back in the Sixties, there was interest in having students think at high levels and to become effective citizens in a turbulent world. The need for high level thinking and authentic world citizens is more crucial now than ever.

Over the years, I have been concerned to develop a theory of educating that would encourage people to move toward fairness and justice in dealing with themselves and others. Authenticity is that common denominator. Authenticity entails thinking about fairness and equality, feeling care for and intimacy with others, and acting through dialogue to understand others and reciprocity to treat them fairly. Within the context of democratic values, movement toward authenticity allows citizens of the world to overcome racism, sexism and other biases with an aim toward creating a better world.

Authentic Educating describes methods that can be used in every discipline and strategies that work in classrooms from elementary to graduate school.

Robert Leahy
DeLand, Florida
July 2008

Permissions

"Corsons Inlet". Copyright © 1963 by A. R. Ammons, from COLLECTED POEMS 1951-1971 by A. R. Ammons. Used by permission of W. W. Norton & Company, Inc.

From I KNOW WHY THE CAGED BIRD SINGS by Maya Angelou, copyright © 1969 and renewed 1997 by Maya Angelou. Used by permission of Random House, Inc.

"since feeling is first". Copyright 1926, 1954, © 1991 by the Trustees for the E. E. Cummings Trust. Copyright © 1985 by George James Firmage, from COMPLETE POEMS: 1904-1962 by E. E. Cummings, edited by George J. Firmage. Used by permission of Liveright Publishing Corporation.

EDUCATING by D.B. Gowin. Copyright © Cornell University Press, 1981. Used by permission of the author.

Ernest Hemingway's Nobel Prize Acceptance Speech, 1954. Copyright © Hemingway Foreign Rights Trust. Reprinted with the permission of Scribner, an imprint of Simon & Schuster Adult Publishing Group, on behalf of the Hemingway Foreign Rights Trust.

THEIR EYES WERE WATCHING GOD by ZORA NEALE HURSTON. Copyright 1937 by Harper & Row, Publishers, Inc.; renewed © 1965 by John C. Hurston and Joel Hurston. Used by permission.

Reprinted with the permission of Scribner, an imprint of Simon & Schuster Adult Publishing Group, from THE COMPLETE POEMS OF MARIANNE MOORE by Marianne Moore. Copyright © 1935 by Marianne Moore; copyright renewed © 1963 by Marianne Moore & T.S. Eliot. All rights reserved.

LEARNING HOW TO LEARN by J. D. Novak & D. B. Gowin. Copyright © Cambridge University Press 1984. Reprinted with the permission of Cambridge University Press.

Educational Philosophy Inventory by R. Leahy from *Becoming a Teacher* by Parkay, F.W. and Stanford, B.H., Copyright © Allyn & Bacon, 1998. Used by permission of the author.

THE HEART OF THOREAU'S JOURNALS by Henry David Thoreau, edited by Odell Shepard. Copyright © 1961 by Dover Publications, Inc. Reprinted with the permission of Dover Publications, Inc.

CHARLOTTE'S WEB by E. B. White. Copyright © 1952 by E. B. White. Text copyright renewed 1980 by E. B. White. Used by permission of HarperCollins Publishers.

Chapter One

Introducing Authentic Educating

For as far back as I can remember I wanted to teach. Luckily, I met many excellent teachers during my somewhat checkered academic career. Because of their influence and example, I work to improve my teaching. In this book, I explain my perspective as *authentic educating*. I write to those already teaching, and those aspiring to teach, because individual teachers transform American education—one life at a time.

When I was a kid, teachers seemed noble, and incredibly lucky. Teachers were noble because they knew so many things and were eager to share. From my kid's perspective, they were lucky because they shared what excited them, enjoyed how it excited their students, and were so well respected in our town that they got paid. They were happily teaching and learning all day, in a shared adventure with students.

For example, I remember making butter from cream by hand in Selma Wassermann's (1993, 2000, 2004) third grade class, back in 1955. I remember our class trip to tour the S.S. United States, then our ride around Manhattan Island on Circle Lines—where my mom, as one of several "class moms", was an enthusiastic chaperone for a group of energetic kids, first through the narrow corridors of the cruise ship, then aboard the decks of the tour boat. From the Circle Lines' deck, as the guide narrated, we saw the Empire State Building, Statue of Liberty, Greenwich Village, Brooklyn Bridge, and the United Nations, with its expansive green lawn and rectangular and curved architecture facing the East River. I was proud when the guide said it was established in New York to work for world peace. Further north, we passed Harlem, where I was born, and the Bronx, where I lived as a kid—until my family moved to Levittown, Long Island, when I was in first grade and where I attended school until graduating from high school in 1965.

Over the years, I had varied success as a student. When I cared about the curriculum, I succeeded. Generally, in courses where the curriculum was not something I cared about, I performed poorly. But when I questioned the teacher's attitude or aims, I learned my most valuable lessons. This happened in classes from junior high school through college, but most memorably during my doctorate at Cornell, in Norman Malcolm's philosophy of mind seminar. Malcolm (1971, 1984) was one of the most celebrated students of the analytic philosopher Ludwig Wittgenstein (1953, 1980)—the Cambridge professor considered by many to be the greatest philosopher of the Twentieth Century.

Professor Malcolm was brilliant and intimidating in the classroom. He controlled discussions with elegant arguments, artful questions, and merciless rebuttals. Back in 1975, he seemed amused by my existentialist inclination toward philosophy as a search for personal meaning, but irritated when I claimed that the German existentialist Martin Heidegger (1962) was considered by many to be the greatest philosopher of the Twentieth Century. Heidegger's ideas about authenticity and care interested me and made analytic philosophy seem pedantic and sterile, which I mentioned in class several times to Malcolm's annoyance. I learned a lot about a philosopher's perspective in Malcolm's class, but clearly not much about what Malcolm wanted me to learn. He recorded the only C on my Cornell transcript, with a comment about how I seemed to pay attention, but did not understand philosophy. See what I mean by a somewhat checkered academic career?

But when I think back to my early experiences and subsequent school successes, the picture I remember is one of sharing an adventure. My experiences through the decades of the Fifties, Sixties, Seventies, Eighties and Nineties and into the New Millennium convince me that what truly counts is the educative relationship between teacher and student. I am writing this book because I believe educational change starts with one teacher and one student at a time in a mutual search for meaning.

One of my favorite teachers, D.B. Gowin defined teaching as sharing meaning in his book *Educating* (1981). I was a graduate student in his philosophy of education seminar at Cornell while he was writing *Educating*. I remember him saying that the one who shares doesn't lose anything, but the one who grasps the shared meaning gains immeasurably. His comment about teaching as sharing meaning helped confirm my belief that teaching is a noble profession. His emphasis on the inherent reciprocity between teacher and learner was a clue to genuine teaching, teaching I experienced at various times throughout my life, something key to authentic educating.

I developed authentic educating with elementary through graduate students and classroom teachers for twenty-five years. This book describes the philosophical basis for authentic educating, particularly in Chapter 2. It contains my Educational Philosophy Inventory (Leahy 1996; Parkay and Stanford 1998) to assess one's educational philosophy. Research indicates that many teachers and aspiring teachers are philosophically supportive of authentic educating. What excites me about authentic educating is working with students and teachers to help them understand concepts from mathematics, to chemistry, to music and language arts in ways that engage them cognitively and emotionally.

After graduating from college, as a science teacher, I was told to help children think at high levels, as indicated in Bloom's Taxonomy, but no one had simple tools to help students do this. Concept maps and learning Vees (Novak and Gowin 1984)—described in Chapters 3 and 4—are tools which guide high level thinking. Not only are they applicable to science, but to every discipline. As described in Chapters 5 and 6, authentic educating gets students emotionally involved in reading literature, analyzing it, writing scripts for plays that they videotape, then edit to demonstrate what they understand. This requires them to work together to show movement of characters toward authenticity in literature from *The Velveteen Rabbit* (1981), *Charlotte's Web* (1999), *Oh, the Places You'll Go* (1990) to *The Old Man and the Sea* (1952), *Huckleberry Finn* (1996) and *I Know Why The Caged Bird Sings* (1993). Students learn the content of the novels, but also become the characters, and work with each other to develop an understanding of their own movement toward authenticity.

Through authentic educating, they learn to think at higher levels, care about others, and interact in ways that enhance what Howard Gardner's theory of multiple intelligences (Eggen and Kauchak 2004) describes as intrapersonal and interpersonal intelligence. Authentic educating helps students to learn on their own and with others, to read and share literature, to interact in a panel presentation format, and as individual presenters using various forms of technology. The value of authentic educating is that it leads toward meaningful educating and personal growth that students find challenging and worthwhile.

I sketched the concepts that form the foundation of my perspective in Figure 1.1: Concept map for authentic educating. This concept map shows the key concepts in a hierarchical network of meaning (Gowin 1981; Novak and Gowin 1984). My philosophic perspective is related to existentialism and progressivism. I explain these and several other contemporary philosophies of education in detail in Chapter 2.

The principles summarized in the concept map are authentic educating:

1. emphasizes personal meaning and responsibility.
2. emphasizes democratic principles to reconstruct experience.
3. uses heuristic tools such as the concept map and learning Vee.

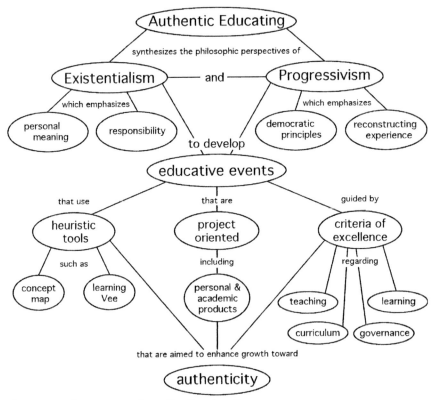

Figure 1.1.   Concept map for authentic educating.

4. is project oriented, including personal and academic products.
5. is guided by criteria of excellence regarding teaching, learning, curriculum and governance.
6. aims to enhance growth toward authenticity.

   The map emphasizes the importance of learning having personal meaning for the student. What a student learns connects directly to what the student knows; one learns new things in relation to past knowledge. For example, a student's knowledge about squares, triangles and circles forms a basis for more sophisticated learning about various angle relationships in plane geometry. The teacher builds on what the student already knows. The student's task is to actively reorganize new meanings with past knowledge. In this way, the student takes responsibility for learning what the teacher shares.
   The existential perspective emphasizes personal meaning and responsibility. The progressive perspective emphasizes the importance of democratic

principles, such as fairness, equality, and humane versus autocratic or harsh treatment in the classroom. The aim is to help students reconstruct experience, that is, to integrate new information with old to enhance problem solving, and to understand how past knowledge connects with future experiences.

These two philosophic perspectives are used to develop educative events—what teachers make happen in the classroom. Authentic educative events use heuristic tools—also called learning tools—such as the concept map, that identifies key concepts in a hierarchical network of meaning and shows relationships among concepts. The second tool is the learning Vee—also called the knowledge or epistemological Vee, so named because of its shape—I use one later in this chapter. The Vee shows the structure, both conceptually and practically, of answers to focus questions in any discipline.

Authentic educative events are project oriented and include personal and academic products. The projects entail students doing and making things. Examples of personal products include: reaction papers, personal journals, concept maps about personal issues, preparing and performing plays, and Vee diagrams that demonstrate learning. Academic products include: essays, term papers, field journals, exams, concept maps to summarize novels and articles, panel presentations and discussions, and Vees. The educative events are guided by criteria of excellence regarding teaching, learning, curriculum and governance. In his theory of educating, Gowin summarizes a key event of educating as "a teacher teaching meaningful materials to a student who grasps the meaning of the materials under humane conditions of social control" (1981, 28).

As I develop authentic educating, I am concerned about the aims of educative events. This entails that one consider what Gowin calls the four commonplaces of educating: teaching, learning, curriculum and governance. These commonplaces need to be considered whenever educating occurs. Educating can occur in an informal setting, like a parent explaining to a child how to set the dinner table for guests. The parent becomes the teacher, the child the learner, appropriate placement of plates and silverware the curriculum, and the parent child relationship the form of governance driving the event. Or it can be the complex professional relationship of a teacher with a class of undergraduate or graduate students discussing the topics, format, writing process, and criteria for evaluation of a term paper. The aim of authentic educating is to enhance growth toward authenticity: a personal attitude to take responsibility for freedom and obligation, to integrate reason and emotion through dialogue, reciprocal recognition, intimacy, and caring as a moral individual (Leahy 1994).

The concept map for authentic educating summarizes and guides this book. To advocate authentic educating is to agree that America is culturally diverse, and to believe in a spirit of respect and common ground within differences such as gender, ethnicity, and religion. The aim is to create authentic relationships that resonate within the principles of democracy upon which this country was founded. These principles of justice and fairness and concern about human rights are contained in the Declaration of Independence and the subsequent revisions of the United States Constitution.

In summary, by definition: authentic educating develops educative events that enhance meaningful learning and growth toward authenticity.

THE CONCEPT OF AUTHENTICITY

The idea that education helps one to establish a voice is fundamental to authentic educating. The idea of voice is central to Carol Gilligan's (1982) and Mary Belenky's (1986) work about women's development. Charles Taylor (1992) emphasized the importance of voice in his book about multiculturalism and political recognition, claiming that human identity is created through dialogue with others. These dialogues are fruitful when they are authentic. The following concept map, see Figure 1.2: Concept map for authenticity, sketches authenticity in a way that connects it to Dewey's and Gowin's theories about education. The concept of authenticity introduced here is developed in the classroom by using characters from literature, then through students assessing their own movement toward authenticity, as they interact with the instructor and each other in classroom activities such as panel discussions, one-act plays, constructing and sharing reaction papers and research papers, assessing their educational philosophy in the public schools through field journals, and sharing personal journal experiences through concept maps that assess their movement toward authenticity.

Authenticity is a personal attitude that aims to take responsibility for choices that involve freedom and obligation. The authentic person views freedom in two fundamental ways: causal and logical. Causal freedom implies that each person is not compelled or coerced to choose. One commits to a choice because one is not simply a product of the environment. For example, many of you reading this book selected teaching as a career from among many possibilities. If the choice fits, you will continue to teach, if not, you would choose another path. Logical freedom implies that the choice an individual makes establishes the moral values in a situation; therefore, a person is morally responsible for choices. By choosing to be a teacher, one chooses to help students learn; helping others is a moral relationship. Authentic freedom in a democratic society means that people are responsible for their choices.

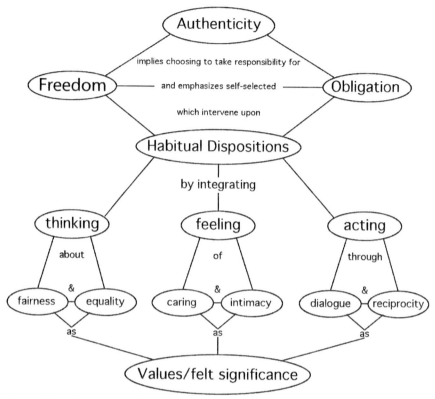

Figure 1.2.   Concept map for authenticity.

The authentic person's attitude toward freedom and obligation intervenes upon his or her habitual dispositions, i.e. one's everyday attitudes toward life. Habits become routine, like brushing one's teeth several times a day, or placing one's keys in a particular place to locate them easily. The habit of authenticity implies that one considers thinking about fairness and equality, that one experiences feelings of care toward others that move toward intimacy— development of emotional closeness with others—that one acts to engage others in meaningful, honest dialogue to develop reciprocal relationships, and that this integration of thinking, feeling and acting becomes routine, as a significant aspect of one's character.

To change a habit requires work. To move routine activities into new awareness entails making changes in ways that freedom and obligation become problematic. For example, when a college student chooses to rent an apartment after living for years at home or in a residence hall, there are many choices that require new habits, like shopping for groceries, preparing meals, or sharing responsibilities for cleaning the apartment. This transition entails a series of choices that reconfigure one's sense of self.

Issues of freedom and obligation intervene upon one's habits. However, in order to change one's habitual dispositions, thinking, feeling and acting are key. Thinking has to do with the way we order ideas. It implies commitment to constructing logical relationships among concepts and giving reasons for our beliefs. One thinks with concepts and images. To be authentic, one must think about fairness and equality. Fairness concerns the informal rules guiding relationships between individuals—formally, in the context of a social contract that guides action in a democracy, fairness guides the meaning of justice (Rawls 1971, 1993, 2001).

These formal rules are contained in what I call the Documents of Freedom and Obligation: the Declaration of Independence and the United States Constitution. At first, our Founding Fathers did not extend their original self-evident truths graciously beyond All (white) men are created equal. Even after the American Revolution, when the Declaration of Independence helped guide the Constitution that took effect in 1789, "We the People" meant We White Males and our White Male posterity. The addition of the Bill of Rights in 1791 provided more protection for white males.

It took years before slaves and women were considered to merit fairness in the formal male documents defining justice, and to have their rights written into the Constitution granting them justice in this society, a justice which continues to evolve as various arguments about fairness are considered in the courts and legislature. Early in our nation's history, women and slaves were not considered to merit equality. The lack of equality was based in part on the belief of the Founding Fathers that women and slaves lacked the ability to reason like white males (Tuana 1992). Therefore, they were denied a place in the social contract; consequently, the original Documents of Freedom and Obligation were inauthentic.

After the Civil War, in 1865 Amendment Thirteen freed slaves, but only former male slaves received the right to vote in 1870, through Amendment Fifteen. It took another fifty years, until 1920, for females to attain a voice through Amendment Nineteen. Another fifty-one years later, with Amendment Twenty-six in 1971, the right to vote was lowered from age twenty-one to eighteen, giving males and females the vote, which is a key aspect to developing an authentic voice in a democracy—or a classroom where students should be allowed certain choices by vote. The relationship between fairness on the individual level and justice on the social contract level is complex, as can be seen in Rawls' development of a theory of justice (1971, 1993, 2001). But as thinking and feeling about equality change in a democracy, change in the formal rules that define justice can move toward authenticity.

Feeling accompanies thinking. Feelings central to authenticity are care and intimacy. Care is primarily concerned with helping the other to grow (Mayeroff 1971). For the philosopher Milton Mayeroff, one is most at home in the world by caring and being cared for, hence, these feeling are central to one's life. As one grows in the ability to care, one also grows in ability to achieve intimacy. In its most significant sense, intimacy is the ability to express oneself honestly and accept the vulnerability it implies in reciprocal relationships (Ferrara 1993).

Combining thinking about fairness and equality with feelings of care and intimacy through dialogue and reciprocity leads toward authenticity. Authentic dialogue requires one to share thoughts about fairness and equality and feelings of care and intimacy. Reciprocity entails that one acknowledges that others have comparable commitment to their personal attitudes and deserve mutual respect, and fair treatment. Therefore, through dialogue and reciprocity, as individuals share thoughts about fairness and equality and feelings of care and intimacy, they develop authentic values. When thinking, feeling and acting merge into authentic values, one feels the significance (Gowin 1981) of this personal integration toward authenticity as one continues to develop authentic relationships with others.

Grounding authentic educating with the concept of authenticity generates a focus for valuable educating. The result is that the individual values authenticity. When thinking and feeling merge, one feels significance; for example, think about taking your driving test to qualify for a license. Try to recall how you felt when you learned that you passed; chances are, that moment, thinking about how a driver's license would change your life merged with your feelings of excitement when you learned that you passed the test and would get a license. Gowin (1981, 43) calls the merging of thinking and feeling "felt significance"—a key element to valuing something. To value authenticity, one must learn that thoughts about fairness and equality, merging with feelings of intimacy and care develop through dialogue and reciprocity. Consider a significant relationship in your life, and reflect on the aspects that make the relationship significant. Think about how you treat the other person fairly and equally, and how you care about the other and achieve intimacy through dialogue and reciprocity—these are the keys to authentic educating.

In conjunction with the educational goals of Dewey and Gowin, authentic educating emphasizes democratic values and personal meaning. For people to develop ability to engage in authentic dialogues is crucial for enhancement of American democracy. Therefore, authentic educating and the concept of authenticity can be of value to aspiring teachers and teachers already in the classroom who want to listen to students' voices in our schools and prepare them for significant lives in America's future and as citizens of the world.

WHY IS AUTHENTIC EDUCATING OF VALUE?

Authentic educating emphasizes self-educating as a goal of education in a democracy. It synthesizes work by two American philosophers of education, John Dewey (1938), a pragmatist and progressive, and D.B. Gowin (1981), an existentialist. Dewey is noted for helping to develop pragmatism, generally believed to be the only indigenous American philosophy. Pragmatism can be traced to methods of problem solving in philosophy and science in the work of Charles Sanders Peirce and William James, and literary antecedents are in works by Ralph Waldo Emerson and Henry David Thoreau.

Dewey was a major influence in American education. He encouraged emphasis on experimental methods in the classroom that led students to increased ability to select and solve problems. His emphasis on education as "continuous reconstruction of experience" (1916, 80) helped guide his distinction between traditional and progressive education. He supported " . . . cultivation of individuality . . . free activity . . . learning through experience . . . making the most of . . . present life . . . and . . . acquaintance with a changing world" (1938, 19-20).

Unfortunately, how others interpreted these suggestions led Dewey to become dissatisfied with how his ideas were misused in schools. Late in his life, he opened his book *Experience & Education* with the claim that "Mankind likes to think in terms of extreme opposites. It is given to formulating its beliefs in terms of Either-Ors, between which it recognizes no intermediate possibilities" (1938, 17). The conflict between traditional and progressive education concerned him. He insisted that progressive education had to be more than abandoning traditional education that imposed external order from above, emphasized isolated skills through drills, arbitrary curriculum content, and a remote future—traditional ideas that still guide much of the essentialist curriculum that drives contemporary schools.

He claimed his approach entailed difficult work. But he insisted the frame of reference was the "organic connection between education and personal experience" (1938, 25) within an experimental philosophy. He aimed to help students to reconstruct their experience by connecting new concepts with old ones in meaningful ways. He wanted to make them better problem solvers and citizens, through educating that involved "both the intellectual and emotional side" (1909, 51). Throughout his writing, he emphasized this new philosophy of educating as a moral enterprise.

As he claimed in his short book *Moral Principles in Education*, "What the normal child continuously needs is not so much isolated moral lessons upon the importance of truthfulness and honesty . . . as the formation of habits of social imagination and conception" (1909, 40). Dewey saw moral education as central to the process and aim of educating, not something tagged on as a list of virtues to recite. Most teachers would probably agree that moral education is important, but many ask, "How do we make moral education a focus of curriculum?" I believe that authentic educating offers answers to this question.

Dewey wrote "just as the material of knowledge is supplied through the senses, so the material of ethical knowledge is supplied by emotional responsiveness" (1909, 52). I believe it is the accuracy of this claim that makes education an inherently moral enterprise. Aristotle believed that sense experience mediated by rational thinking established knowledge, and Dewey advocated use of the scientific method to evaluate sense experience and support knowledge claims. But they both agreed that reason and emotion are involved in ethical action. That education involves intellect and emotion in a social context shows why Kohlberg's (Parkay 1998) theory of moral development seemed at first promising but then open to criticism.

The initial appeal of Kohlberg's six level scale, two stages in each of three levels: pre-conventional, conventional and post conventional, was established by assessing reasoned responses to hypothetical moral dilemmas. To implement his theory about moral development into the schools, teachers discussed his theory of moral development and used various hypothetical moral dilemmas that Kohlberg developed while he tested his theory. Unfortunately for Kohlberg's approach, moral education does not involve only reasoning ability, nor can it be accomplished by having students discuss only hypothetical examples. Developing students' reasoning ability is neither sufficient for moral education, nor does discussing hypothetical situations engage student's emotions with genuine moral problems. Dewey's claim that moral education requires an integration of intellect and emotions seems on target.

As Gilligan (1982) claimed in her criticism of Kohlberg's theory of moral development, for women, care is central to moral action. However, subsequent emphasis on the centrality of caring (Noddings 1984) as a foundation for a separate feminine approach to ethics and moral education seems to eliminate men. I find it ironic that Noddings based much of her work about caring on "a lovely little book, *On Caring*" (1984, 9) by Milton Mayeroff, but then developed his ideas into a feminine approach.

As an undergraduate student in Mayeroff's existentialism class during the late Sixties, when he was writing *On Caring* (1971), my belief was that he was exploring the concept of caring philosophically, intending it to apply to both men and women. As Mayeroff wrote in his introduction, "In the sense in which a man can ever be said to be at home in the world, he is at home not through dominating, or explaining, or appreciating, but through caring and being cared for" (1971, 3). Granted, that was during the sexist olden days, when "man" was used as a universal pronoun. But I believe he was talking to both young men and women in our class when he insisted that caring can give "comprehensive meaning and ordering to one's life" (1971, 3). It seemed to me then, and still does, that he was making an existential claim about the human condition. From a practical viewpoint, caring helps one make meaning of one's life. I believe he meant that both men and women should order their lives through caring.

The argument that there is a male ethic versus a female ethic has deep roots in philosophy. It seems to rest upon the belief that justice is based on the ability to reason autonomously, and that women do not have sufficient reasoning ability (Tuana 1992; Leahy 1994). Development of an ethic of care by women writers aims to find new ground for the moral development of women by making a distinction between men and women. But the book by Katz, Noddings and Strike, *Justice and Caring: The Search for Common Ground in Education* (1999) focuses on reaching common ground between these two approaches.

Ken Strike—another excellent teacher I met as a graduate student at Cornell—wrote masterfully in this book about the strengths and weaknesses of these two approaches. The justice argument emphasizes reasons and rules. The caring argument emphasizes emotion and relationships.

When I was a graduate student in one of his seminars, I remember Ken said, "As a philosopher, when in doubt, make a distinction." He did it well in this book, when he wrote: "I argue that the view that sees justice and caring as deeply different . . . is wrong and that an account of the tension between justice and caring rooted in moral pluralism is more defensible" (1999, 23). Strike continues to lean toward the justice argument as more comprehensive, but he claims "appreciation of moral complexity that moral pluralism affords may be an aid in promoting tolerance and reciprocity" (1999, 36). Pluralism implies there are various accounts of what morality implies, but I believe the search for common ground should promote education that helps students understand justice and caring, and learn to balance reason and emotion. Helping students to understand and achieve this balance that promotes tolerance and reciprocity is key to authentic educating.

Dewey's balanced approach to moral education, one that attempts to integrate reason and emotion to help students toward good judgment, suggests that there is an experiential component needed. The child develops judgment by making and testing judgments. "He must have an opportunity to select for himself, and to attempt to put his selections into execution, that he may submit them to the final test, that of action" (Dewey 1909, 55). There is an ominous tone to the word execution, given the rash of violence in American schools recently. But clearly, the aim of moral education should be toward reducing violence. It should attempt to integrate student thinking and feeling into moral action. Students involved in school violence seem to have not integrated their feeling and thinking. They act out of indifference or anger, with little thought about the consequences.

Unfortunately, many violent students appear like the odd character Meursault in Nobel Prize winning author Albert Camus' *The Stranger* (1946)—a novel Mayeroff had us read in his existentialism class in 1968. Meursault acknowledged his emotional detachment during his murder trial stating simply that he no longer noted his feelings. But he gave no more explanation for his random act of violence than that the sun was in his eyes. His lack of emotional integration seems to foreshadow the profile of many students committing violence in our contemporary schools. Meursault's emotional fragmentation symbolizes that a student's emotional integration should be a focus of worthwhile education.

There is no amount of gun sweeps, locker checks or metal detectors that will eliminate occasional random violence. It would be naïve to think authentic educating would end violence in schools. There are too many factors involved to stop high-profile media-attracting heirs to Meursault. However, I believe if teachers aim to learn more about how their students think and feel, many more troubled students would be found and helped, and the overwhelming majority of students, good kids genuinely struggling with life's complexities, could be better educated.

Moral principles are essential to educating. "They are inherent in community life, and in the working structure of the individual" (Dewey 1909, 58). I agree with Dewey that we can have faith in these facts. As teachers, we are caretakers of community life. This implies that as teachers, we ought to intervene in students' lives to help them become contributing members of the community. Dewey claimed that teachers who believe moral principles are key to education "will find every subject, every method of instruction, every incident of school life pregnant with moral possibility" (1909, 58).

Unfortunately, he ended his book there—emphasizing moral possibility. So, we teachers must figure out what to do. But an example of bad teaching that he developed early in the book lingers in my mind, hinting toward a direction. He offered as an example, someone teaching swimming without using water. As Dewey dryly acknowledged, when a student trained to swim without water was asked what happened when he got into the water "he laconically replied, 'Sunk'" (1909, 14). Just as it seems impossible to learn to swim outside water, so it seems moral education that does not involve the real world of students' experience is equally futile.

We need to do more as educators with moral possibility. It should be central to what we do. I believe as teachers, our philosophy of educating guides what we do in the classroom. Research conducted using my Educational Philosophy Inventory (Leahy 1996) suggests that the majority of teachers and students majoring in education hold philosophic perspectives consistent with progressivism and existentialism, although much of curriculum seems driven by essentialism—a view held by many legislators, but only a minority of teachers. As I mentioned earlier, authentic educating blends pragmatism that Dewey developed into progressivism, existentialism that drives Mayeroff's book about caring, and tools from Gowin's theory of educating. I want to show how authentic educating makes moral possibility central.

Figure 1.3: Vee for authentic educating uses a second heuristic tool to ask and answer the question that guides this section, "Why is Authentic Educating of Value?" The Vee heuristic, like the concept map, organizes knowledge into a hierarchy. On the left side is the theoretical/conceptual framework used to answer a focus question. A conceptual framework starts, at the lowest level, by naming an event with key concepts. To answer my question, I define and assess events of authentic educating. Key concepts, when related to each other, form principles; and principles, when self-supporting and useful, lead to a theory. The next more comprehensive conceptual level is philosophy.

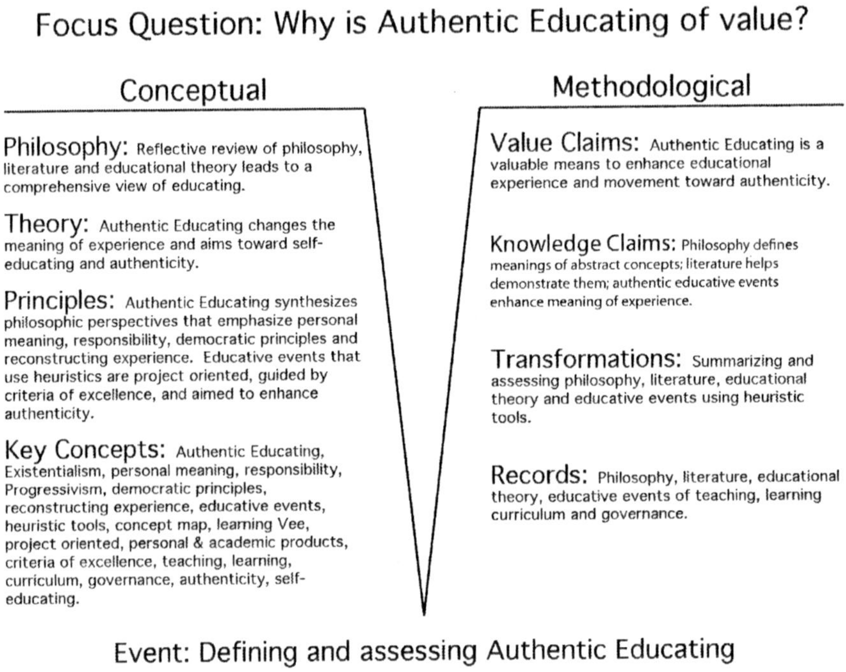

Focus Question: Why is Authentic Educating of value?

Conceptual

Philosophy: Reflective review of philosophy, literature and educational theory leads to a comprehensive view of educating.

Theory: Authentic Educating changes the meaning of experience and aims toward self-educating and authenticity.

Principles: Authentic Educating synthesizes philosophic perspectives that emphasize personal meaning, responsibility, democratic principles and reconstructing experience. Educative events that use heuristics are project oriented, guided by criteria of excellence, and aimed to enhance authenticity.

Key Concepts: Authentic Educating, Existentialism, personal meaning, responsibility, Progressivism, democratic principles, reconstructing experience, educative events, heuristic tools, concept map, learning Vee, project oriented, personal & academic products, criteria of excellence, teaching, learning, curriculum, governance, authenticity, self-educating.

Methodological

Value Claims: Authentic Educating is a valuable means to enhance educational experience and movement toward authenticity.

Knowledge Claims: Philosophy defines meanings of abstract concepts; literature helps demonstrate them; authentic educative events enhance meaning of experience.

Transformations: Summarizing and assessing philosophy, literature, educational theory and educative events using heuristic tools.

Records: Philosophy, literature, educational theory, educative events of teaching, learning curriculum and governance.

Event: Defining and assessing Authentic Educating

Figure 1.3.   Vee for authentic educating.

The learning Vee requires that the conceptual framework constructed on the left side is supported on the right side by testable methods and evidence. The methodological side requires accurate record keeping about the question and events under consideration. By summarizing records, called transformations of records into meaningful patterns, one can make knowledge and value claims.

My philosophy claim in the Vee is that "Reflective review of philosophy, literature and educational theory leads to a comprehensive view of educating." My research in classrooms during the past twenty-five years leads to the value claim that "Authentic Educating is a valuable means to enhance educational experience and movement toward authenticity." Authentic educating offers practical methods for meaningful learning, and a philosophic aim that encourages development of values key to participants in a democratic society.

I hope that authentic educating will appeal to many teachers. The emphasis in this perspective is upon the importance of personal meaning, both in terms of how new concepts fit into the student's previous conceptual framework, and concepts that are significant to the learner. The other key is that each student has responsibility in learning. Learning is an active process of integrating new meanings with old, and the teacher cannot do this for the student. The student must take charge of learning what the teacher shares. The teacher cannot learn for the student. Learning is the student's responsibility.

Much like one could not hand a pencil to a student unless the student was intent on grasping hold of it, learning requires a student's readiness to grasp concepts. But then the student must take responsibility to actively reorganize or rehearse the new concepts to actually learn them. Learning is like doing something with a pencil after grasping it.

This two-pronged approach—to make concepts meaningful by connecting them with previous knowledge and to emphasize their significance to the student—puts responsibility on teacher and student. The teacher needs to share concepts effectively and efficiently. Teachers should select curriculum that is important and meaningful to students, so students may take responsibility for learning and feel the significance of it. According to Gowin "A powerful moment in educating occurs when grasping the meaning and feeling the significance come together" (1981, 43). Gowin called this merging of thinking and feeling felt significance. He emphasized it as a fundamental value in educating.

Getting students to feel the significance of what they are learning is a challenge for teachers. The challenge requires selecting excellent materials, then teaching in a way that captures students' interests and connects with their lives. It can be done. My examples of Wassermann's class projects and field trips, Mayeroff sharing manuscript pages from *On Caring*, and comments by Gowin and Strike are experiences that remain with me—as has my poor grade in Professor Malcolm's seminar. These events had felt significance for me. I continue to value them as they influence my teaching.

These days, in the field journal assignment for my foundations of education course, I have students contact a teacher who affected their lives. They let the teacher know that they are considering a teaching career, partly because of that teacher's influence. Students are surprised to find an extremely high coincidence of shared philosophies of education with teachers they contact (Leahy 1996). Think about excellent teachers you have known. A little reminiscing will bring to mind powerful examples of felt significance. Chances are these educative events were exciting for both teacher and student. Equally likely, these events continue to influence your philosophy of education, and do or will affect your teaching. Most likely, they are events of authentic educating.

Chapter Two

Developing a
Philosophy of Education

How one teaches depends upon one's philosophy of educating. In Chapter 1, I said that authentic educating fits closely with the educational philosophies of existentialism and progressivism. In this chapter, I sketch an overview of philosophy and several popular educational philosophies. But first, the following self-scoring *Educational Philosophy Inventory* (Leahy 1996; Parkay 1995) will help to identify your personal philosophy.

EDUCATIONAL PHILOSOPHY INVENTORY

The following inventory is provided to help identify your educational philosophy. Respond to each statement on a scale from 5 "Strongly Agree" to 1 "Strongly Disagree" by circling the number that most closely fits your perspective.

For example, the first item states "The curriculum should emphasize a fixed set body of knowledge *not* students' personal interests." Do you believe that curriculum should emphasize a set fixed body of knowledge? Or do you believe that curriculum should focus on students' personal interests? If you believe curriculum should be the same for all students, you probably "strongly agree" with the first item. If you believe there should be a balance between a set curriculum and students' interests, you would probably select "3", in the middle. If you believe that students' personal interests should be the major consideration in planning curriculum, you probably "strongly disagree" with the first statement. In items containing a *not*, you are being asked to consider with which part of the statement you most strongly agree then express your reaction to the whole statement with a number that most closely identifies your preference.

As you read the items, you may feel that many concepts are abstract and that educators have pondered them for centuries. Do not try to solve these items, simply record a number that accounts for how you react to them, based on your understanding of the abstract words and how you believe education should be. After you complete the self-scoring section at the end, read the short descriptions of the philosophic perspectives to see which most closely fit your views. Record a 5, 4, 3, 2, or 1 for each item (5 indicates *Strongly Agree* and 1 indicates *Strongly Disagree*):

1. The curriculum should emphasize a set fixed body of knowledge *not* students' personal interests.
2. All learning results from rewards controlled by the external environment.
3. Teachers should emphasize interdisciplinary subject matter that encourages project oriented, democratic classrooms.
4. Education should emphasize the search for personal meaning, *not* a set fixed body of knowledge.
5. The ultimate aim of education is constant, absolute, and universal: to cultivate the rational intellect.
6. Schools should actively involve students in social change to reform society.
7. Schools should teach basic skills *not* humanistic ideals.
8. Eventually human behavior will be explained by scientific laws proving there is no free will.
9. Teachers should be facilitators and resources who guide student inquiry *not* managers of behavior.
10. The best teachers encourage personal responses and develop self-awareness of their students.
11. The curriculum should be the same for everyone: the collective wisdom of Western culture delivered through lecture and discussion.
12. Schools should lead society toward radical social change *not* transmit traditional values.
13. The purpose of schools is to ensure practical preparation for life *not* to encourage personal choice.
14. The best teachers manage student behavior efficiently and accurately measure learning of prescribed objectives.
15. Curriculum should emerge from students' needs and interests, therefore it *should not* be prescribed in advance.
16. Helping students develop personal values is more important than transmitting traditional values.
17. The best education would consist primarily of exposure to great works in the humanities.

18. It is more important for teachers to involve students in activities to criticize and transform society than to teach the "Great Books."
19. Schools should emphasize discipline, hard work, and respect for authority *not* reform society.
20. Human learning can be controlled: anyone can be taught to be a scientist or a thief; therefore personal choice is a myth.
21. Education should enhance personal growth through problem solving in the present *not* emphasize preparation for a distant future.
22. Since we are born with an unformed personality, personal growth should be the focus of education.
23. The universal constant in human nature is the ability to reason, therefore the sole focus of education should be to develop reasoning ability.
24. Schools perpetuate racism and sexism camouflaged as traditional values.
25. Teachers should efficiently transmit a set fixed body of knowledge *not* experiment with curriculum.
26. Teaching is primarily management of student behavior to achieve the teacher's objectives.
27. Education should involve students in democratic activities and reflective thinking.
28. Students should have significant involvement in choosing what and how they learn.
29. Teachers should promote the permanency of the "classics" *not* practical preparation for life.
30. Learning should lead students to involvement in social reform.
31. On the whole, school should and must indoctrinate students with traditional values.
32. If ideas cannot be proved by science, they should be ignored as superstition and nonsense.
33. The major goal for teachers is to create an environment where students can learn on their own by guided reflection upon their experiences.
34. Teachers should create opportunities for students to make personal choices *not* shape their behavior.
35. The aim of education should be the same in every age and society *not* differ from teacher to teacher.
36. Education should lead society toward social betterment *not* practical preparation for life.

EPI Score Sheet: Record the number you circled for each statement (1-36). Total the number for each perspective's statements and record it. The highest total indicates your educational philosophy.

Essentialism: Essentialism was a response to progressivism. It advocates a conservative philosophic perspective. The emphasis is on intellectual and moral standards that should be transmitted by schools. The core of the curriculum should be essential knowledge and skills. Schooling should be practical and not influence social policy. It is a "back to basics" movement, which emphasizes facts. Students should be taught discipline, hard work, and respect for authority. Influential essentialists: William Bagley, H.G. Rickover, Arthur Bestor, William Bennett; E.D. Hirsch's *Cultural Literacy* could fit this category. (Statements 1; 7; 13; 19; 25; 31)

Behaviorism: Behaviorists deny free will and maintain that behavior is the result of external forces, which cause humans to behave in predictable ways. Behaviorism is linked with empiricism, which stresses scientific experiment and observation. Behaviorists are skeptical about metaphysical claims. Behaviorists look for laws governing human behavior the way natural scientists look for empirical laws governing natural events. The role of the teacher is to identify behavioral goals and establish a reward system to achieve goals. Influential behaviorists: B.F. Skinner, Ivan Pavlov, J.B. Watson, Benjamin Bloom. (Statements 2; 8; 14; 20; 26; 32)

Progressivism: Progressivism focuses more on the child than the subject matter. The students' interests and personal growth are important. Learners should be active and learn to solve problems by reflecting upon their experience. The school should help students develop democratic personal and social values. Because society is always changing, new ideas are important to make the future better than the past. Influential progressives: John Dewey, William Kilpatrick, Francis Parker. (Statements 3; 9; 15; 21; 27; 33)

Existentialism: Existentialism is a highly subjective philosophy that stresses the importance of the individual and emotional commitment to living authentically. It emphasizes individual choice over the importance of rational theories, history, and social institutions. Jean Paul Sartre, the French philosopher, claimed "Existence precedes essence." Sartre meant that people are born and must define themselves through personal choices. Influential existentialists: Jean Paul Sartre, Soren Kierkegaard, Martin Buber, Martin Heidegger, Gabriel Marcel, Friedrich Nietzsche, Albert Camus, Carl Rogers, A.S. Neill, and Maxine Greene. (Statements 4; 10; 16; 22; 28; 34)

Perennialism: Perennialists advocate that the aim of education is to ensure that students acquire knowledge about the great ideas of Western culture. Human beings are rational, and it is this capacity that needs to be developed.

Cultivation of the intellect is the highest priority of an education worth having. The highest level of knowledge in each field should be the focus of curriculum. Influential perennialists are: Robert Maynard Hutchins, Mortimer Adler, Allan Bloom. (Statements 5; 11; 17; 23; 29; 35)

Reconstructionism: Reconstructionists advocate that schools should take the lead to reconstruct society. Schools have more than a responsibility to transmit knowledge they have the mission to transform society as well. Reconstructionists go beyond progressivists in advocating social activism. Influential reconstructionists: Theodore Brameld, George Counts, Paulo Friere, Henry Giroux. (Statements 6; 12; 18; 24; 30; 36)

Source: Robert Leahy from Parkay's *Becoming a Teacher*, Allyn & Bacon, 1995.

Your responses to the Inventory probably favor several philosophic perspectives. Look at your highest and lowest scores. The high scores indicate those perspectives most consistent with your views about teaching, learning, curriculum and governance: the four commonplaces of educating. For example, in question 1, if you believe the curriculum should emphasize "a set fixed body of knowledge," you probably scored high in essentialism. If you believe curriculum should emphasize "students' personal interests," you probably scored high in progressivism. But, before summarizing the philosophies of education identified in the Inventory in more detail in a later section, there is a brief introduction to philosophy in the following section.

WHAT IS PHILOSOPHY AND WHAT DOES IT HAVE TO DO WITH EDUCATION?

To define philosophy for elementary school students (or undergraduate and graduate students unfamiliar with philosophy), I translate "philo" from Greek to mean "love of" and "sophia" to mean "wisdom." To clarify what it means to be a philosopher, I quote from Thoreau's *Walden*, "To be a philosopher is not merely to have subtle thoughts, nor even to found a school, but so to love wisdom as to live according to its dictates a life of simplicity, independence, magnanimity, and trust" (1993, 12). Then, to help elementary school students remember the branches of philosophy, I ask them to recite the word "meal" as a mnemonic tool: metaphysics, epistemology, axiology, and logic.

Metaphysics, which translates as "beyond physics" (Knight 1998, 15), is about how philosophers consider issues regarding the ultimate nature of reality. Questions such as: how did the universe begin, does God exist, or what is the nature of being human, or are humans by nature disposed toward creating cultural groups are metaphysical questions that consider the meaning of life and the aims and purposes of human beings. Questions regarding the origin and purpose of the universe are considered in the study (ology) of the cosmos: cosmology. The German philosopher, Martin Heidegger, for example, in his book *Being and Time* (1959), considered the ontological question "What is the nature of human being?" Questions about the nature and existence of God are considered in theology. Questions about the origin of culture, or the existence of free will, or whether humans are inherently good or evil are considered in anthropology.

Epistemology, from the Greek "episteme" which translates as "knowledge" and, again, "ology" the "study of", is key to philosophy. The central concern in epistemology is how we can justify what we claim to be knowledge. Throughout the history of philosophy there has been a range of ways to justify knowledge claims.

Axiology, as I tell elementary students, has nothing to do with "axes"— except, maybe, how to use one—but is the study of values. The major values studied are ethics, those that have to do with right and wrong with regard to treating others, and aesthetics, those values that have to do with beauty and art. Axiology is important in education because ethics is the focus of how we treat each other, including how teachers treat students and vice versa, and how students treat each other. With regard to authentic educating, the key values are those of fairness and caring, so ethical considerations are important in the classroom. Aesthetics are important in education also. What we have students read in various courses entails aesthetic considerations. How we define what makes a "good" piece of literature, or a good painting or piece of music for students to learn involves axiological decisions about aesthetics.

The final branch, logic, has to do with assessing correct and incorrect reasoning. Logic involves evaluation of propositions involved in arguments, to assess the premises and inferences to determine whether the arguments are valid. Valid arguments can then be assessed as sound—meaning that the argument is valid and the premises are true. In conjunction with epistemological claims, one can assess the truth of propositions within the argument, thus establishing arguments as sound. The history of logic can be traced back almost twenty-five hundred years to the Greek philosopher Aristotle, who identified forms of valid arguments and the nature of illogical arguments called fallacies. In the 19th and 20th centuries, logic became a focus for not only philosophers, but mathematicians such as Bertrand Russell and Alfred North Whitehead, especially in their book *Principia Mathematica*. See Figure 2.1: Concept map for branches of philosophy.

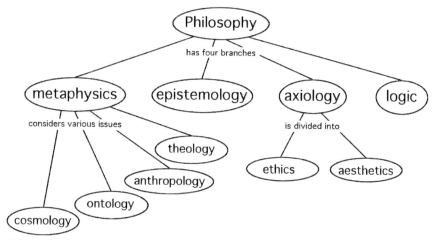

Figure 2.1.   Concept map for branches of philosophy.

Epistemology entails three aspects: the dimensions of truth and various perspectives that address truth, the sources of knowledge, and theories that attempt to confirm the validity of knowledge. The various perspectives that have developed in philosophy include skepticism, which ranges from belief that humans can know nothing for certain, to a more limited skepticism that implies a questioning attitude, often attributed to scientists, that doubt is justified until there is evidence to support a claim. In regard to theological questions, such as about the nature and existence of God, the perspective of agnosticism implies a belief that humans are unable to know with any certainty about the existence of spiritual beings, since humans live in a material world of sense experience. With regard to truth, there are those, like Plato, who claim truth to be absolute, permanent and universal. In contrast, the scientific method implies a relativist position, with an underlying assumption that as evidence is accumulated, accuracy of claims is substantiated, but further evidence may refute an established claim, such that, in the scientific community, truth is in flux.

However, it seems that most scientists believe that truth is external to the individual; the scientific method is the attempt to ascertain this knowledge as objective. Others see knowledge as an interaction between the external world and humans. Then there are those who believe that knowledge is a human construction and there are no grounds for claiming knowledge is external, objective, universal or eternal. These folks consider knowledge as subjective and tend toward the arts and literature (Knight 1998).

The final dimension is of those who claim that truth is built into the nature of reality. They believe truth exists apart from human beings, and in some way is built into the nature of the mind, therefore, truth is prior to experience, and called *a priori* knowledge. Kant, for example, seemed to believe that the human mind had categories, such as cause and effect, implying that "instead of thinking of our knowledge as conforming to a realm of objects, we think of objects as conforming to our ways of knowing" (Honderich 1995, 436). In contrast, knowledge that depends upon human experience for verification is called *a posteriori* knowledge.

When it comes to the sources of knowledge, philosophers like Aristotle claimed that it comes through our senses of touch, taste, sight, hearing and smell, and that we reason about our experience to mediate claims about what we know. Others claim that revelation is the most important source of knowledge. "Believers in revelation hold that this form of knowledge has the distinct advantage of being an omniscient source of information" (Knight 1998, 22) and, therefore, is absolute, and not refutable by empirical (sense) data. An additional source of truth is that of authority, generally, an expert in a particular field. "In the classroom, the most common source of information is some authority, such as a textbook, teacher, or reference work" (1998, 22). When reason guides knowledge, the perspective is called "rationalism". The claim is that reason and logic can guide the mind toward truth. Intuition is a source of immediate personal certainty, or insight, that people claim as guides to truth.

In philosophy, there are three prominent approaches to assessing the validity of knowledge claims. In the correspondence theory, the test is to establish as fact circumstances that can be empirically verified. For example, to claim that the Loch Ness Monster exists, the burden of proof is to offer empirical evidence—only Nessie herself would count. The coherence theory relies upon the belief that a statement needs to be consistent with related statements. The pragmatic theory, which asserts that truth is not absolute, claims that the test of truth is "its utility, workability, or satisfactory consequences. In the thinking of John Dewey and William James, truth is what works" (Knight 1998, 25). Critics of the pragmatic theory claim that inevitably, it leads to relativism—what is true for Smith may be false for Jones, without a method to resolve the differences. Clearly, each of the three approaches to validity is flawed to critics. See Figure 2.2: Concept map for epistemology.

The following concept map (Figure 2.3) summarizes the branches of philosophy, the major philosophic perspectives, and philosophers related to the particular philosophic perspectives. A philosophic perspective addresses questions regarding metaphysics, epistemology, axiology and logic. Plato, considered as the developer of idealism—best thought of as "idea-ism": the

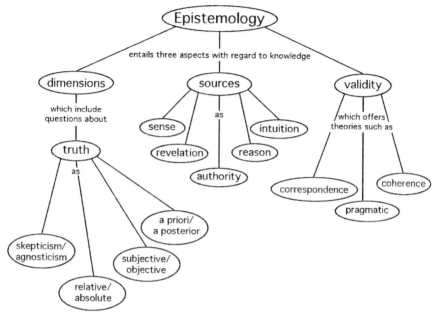

Figure 2.2.   Concept map for epistemology.

belief in the permanence and truth of ideas—argued in his book *The Republic* (Cornford 1945) that the mind could grasp that truth is permanent. In his Allegory of the Cave, he argued that true knowledge was permanent, contained in the Forms—for example, we identify a particular tree because we grasp how it is similar to the concept of tree that we have in our mind. Since the senses can make mistakes, Plato argued that only the mind, when correctly trained, could grasp truth. His student Aristotle disagreed with the existence of the ideal world of the Forms and argued for reason assessing the senses as a better arbiter of truth. Two thousand years later, the pragmatists, Pierce, James and Dewey argued for the validity of experimental methods to achieve truth. The existentialists, on the other hand, argued that the important truths were subjective and defined what makes life meaningful.

Generally, idealism and realism are considered the major traditional approaches to philosophy, whereas pragmatism and existentialism are considered modern philosophies (Knight 1998). But each of the four perspectives has influenced a range of philosophers over the years, and these influences are felt in education as the following concept map indicates (Figure 2.4). Realism influenced behaviorists, logical positivists, and analytic philosophers like Wittgenstein in the Twentieth Century. Aspects of realism combined with idealist notions influenced Mortimer Adler and Robert Hutchins in their

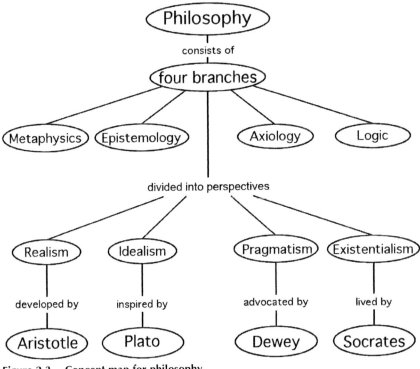

Figure 2.3.   Concept map for philosophy.

development of perennialism, whereas, many essentialists relied heavily on idealism to argue for absolute truths and the authority of curriculum based on such truths. Dewey's pragmatic philosophy influenced the progressive movement in the schools, and led his students at Columbia to develop the perspective of reconstructionism.

Other philosophic perspectives influence contemporary education: post-modernism, deconstruction, critical pedagogy, etc. Where the future will lead remains to be seen.

PHILOSOPHIES OF EDUCATION

In the remainder of this chapter, I summarize six popular philosophic per-spectives in education identified in the inventory, using student concept maps developed as class assignments in courses about philosophy of educa-tion. The student concept maps demonstrate the students' comprehension of their readings from sections of Parkay and Stanford's *Becoming a Teacher*

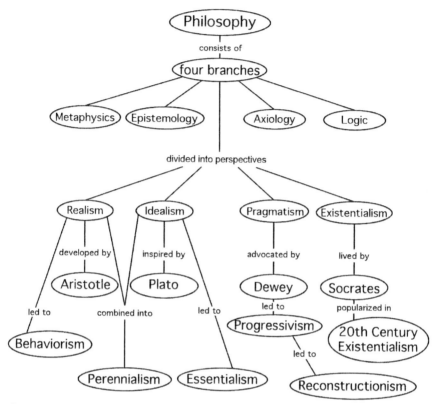

Figure 2.4. Concept map for philosophy of education.

(1998), Knight's *Issues & Alternatives in Educational Philosophy* (1998) that summarizes key concepts from philosophy and philosophy of education, and Cahn's *Classic and Contemporary Readings in the Philosophy of Education* (1997) that contains excerpts from writings by outstanding philosophers in the history of philosophy, such as Plato, Aristotle, Locke, Rousseau, Kant, and Dewey, and articles by contemporary philosophers of education, such as Amy Gutmann, Paulo Freire, Nel Noddings, Maxine Greene, Richard Rorty and others. Most of the maps were constructed in PowerPoint that students presented in class for discussion of various sections of the texts (all student work is used by permission).

Essentialism

This perspective developed during the 1930s, as a reaction against progressivism. These educators disagreed with what they saw as the drift away from mastery of basic skills. They believed school should be a place that emphasized basic facts and stricter discipline. It is a conservative position that does not see the aim of schools to be child-centered in a way that distracts attention from a core curriculum.

In the 1930s William Bagley, Isaac Kandel and Frederick Breed organized an Essentialist Committee that intended to establish a direction for American education aimed away from the progressive ideas of the time. Essentialist ideas were the focus of another organization in the 1950s, with Mortimer Smith and Arthur Bestor as key spokesmen. Bestor's discontent with schools was quite clearly evident in the titles of his books, for example "*Educational Wastelands: The Retreat from Learning in Our Public Schools*" (Knight 1998, 113). Bestor was concerned that rigor was declining in the curriculum and classroom, replaced by activities that had little educational value. The following map summarizes aspects of essentialism from Knight (1998) (Figure 2.5).

This discontent with schools heightened after the Russian launch of the Sputnik satellite in October 1957. Deep in the Cold War, the Sputnik launch was taken as a military threat to this country. As a fifth grade student, it seemed to me that the Russian space success was perceived as American educational failure; the result was a monumental effort to revise school curriculum to emphasize patriotic involvement in math and science. So, as important as it was for America to defeat Germany in Berlin in 1936 to denounce Hitler's myth of the Aryan race, it was crucial for American athletes to defeat Russian athletes at the Olympics scheduled for Rome in 1960 to prove the superiority of American society, but it seemed more important to have American students dedicated to defeating Russian students in a core curriculum of math and science, in order to assure the survival of our society.

As our space program attempted to catch-up with the Russians, by launching the sub-orbital flight of Alan Shepard on May 5, 1961—that with class-

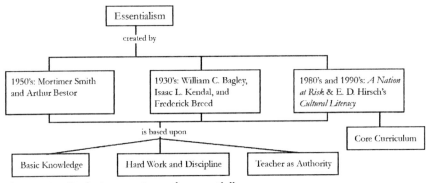

Figure 2.5. Student concept map for essentialism.

mates, I listened to nervously as it was broadcast over the school public address system in my eighth grade art class—concern about the rigor of the curriculum continued because Yuri Gagarin had been the first man to orbit Earth on April 1961. The orbital flight of John Glenn in February 1962 still meant America was behind, and math and science in school were critical for the survival of the United States. Not until Neil Armstrong's moonwalk July 21, 1969 could Americans declare space superiority. But by then, during the height of the Vietnam War, schools were immersed in a different move-ment—various forms of rebellion advocating broadly humanistic aims—that soon brought an invigorated essentialist call for "back to basics."

In 1983, when the National Commission on Excellence in Education pub-lished *A Nation at Risk*, once again there was clamor to return to basics. The Commission feared the "rising tide of mediocrity that threatened our very future as a Nation" (Knight 1998, 114). The Commission outlined a core cur-riculum for high school graduation that included four years of English and three years of math, science and social studies, with a half year dedicated to computer science.

The essentialist argument continues in the schools. E.D. Hirsch's book *Cultural Literacy* (1988) lists "5,000 essential names, phrases, dates, and concepts" in its appendix titled "What Literate Americans Know." Samples on the back cover of his book include such items as "absolute zero, Alamo, Homestead Act, Icarus, *tabula rasa*, Valhalla, Battle of Waterloo, Zeitgeist." In subsequent work, Hirsch established the Core Knowledge Foundation and edited a series of books for use in elementary schools. There were six volumes in the Core Knowledge Series by 1996, with titles like *What Your First Grader Needs to Know*. By the late Nineties, several hundred schools adopted his basic principles and implemented aspects of his Core Knowledge (Knight 1998, 116).

Hirsch continues the essentialist tradition. The essentialists emphasize basic knowledge. Hirsch has identified key concepts for the curriculum and wants students to know them. Literacy and basic math are key to the essen-tialist curriculum. At the secondary level, curriculum outlined in *Nation at Risk* continues to be central.

Generally, it is dissatisfaction with performance of students on knowledge considered "core" that upsets the essentialists. I find that students of mine who score as existentialists and progressives on the inventory, after they go out as undergraduates to do field experience in local schools, come back with greater respect for essentialist concerns. After ten hours of observing in the schools, they worry that many students lack basic knowledge and skills.

Essentialists tend to believe that "learning is hard work and requires dis-cipline" (Knight, 116). Essentialists believe there are things students need to know. As Hirsch says in his preface, "literacy requires the early and continued transmission of specific information. Dewey was deeply mistaken to disdain 'accumulating information in the form of symbols'" (Hirsch 1988, xvii). Here we see the essentialist argument *for* a core curriculum and *against* Dewey; although it is doubtful that Dewey advocated illiteracy or that he should be blamed for how others misused his ideas. Anyway, essentialists tend to argue for emphasis on content. "Cultural literacy is represented not by a *prescriptive* list of books but rather by a *descriptive* list of the information actually possessed by literate Americans" (Hirsch 1988, xiv). A key concern about what information literate Americans possess is how they came to possess it: doubtful it was by rote memorization of lists of information. Therefore, a concern about essentialism is about what methods are used to get students to learn what is contained in the core curriculum.

Essentialist learning techniques tend to emphasize memorization and drill. The knowledge is prescribed in advance, and the student's task is to accumulate it. This implies that the teacher is the authority in the classroom, with regard to knowledge and classroom management. The teacher is to be respected for both knowledge and as disciplinarian. Essentialism is a reaction against the liberal ideas of Dewey that essentialists considered soft and the aristocratic ideas of the perennialists, who advocated a curriculum dedicated to reading and discussion of the "Great Books."

Behaviorism

If you believe that learning is a result of external control, either through rewards or punishments, you probably scored high in behaviorism. You probably agree that eventually, human behavior will be explained through scientific laws. In the classroom, the teacher should manage students' behavior efficiently, and accurately measure how well the students learn the prescribed objectives. Also, you probably agree that any student, in the correctly controlled environment, can achieve the teacher's objectives.

Historically, this perspective is attributed to the work of the Russian psychologist Ivan Pavlov (1849-1936), who worked with dogs to develop the techniques of classical conditioning. Behaviorism was popularized in the United States through the work of John Watson (1878-1958) and B.F. Skinner (1904-1990) (Parkay 1998). Two of Skinner's major works were his novel *Walden Two* (1948), about implementing behavioral engineering into a Utopian community, and a philosophic piece titled *Beyond Freedom and Dignity* (1971). In these works, he emphasized that the concept of free will was an illusion, a remnant from pre-scientific notions. He claimed that the environment shapes our behavior through outside forces. People repeat behaviors that are reinforced. Since free will amounts to people doing what they want, when they are reinforced, they are doing what they want, and the concept of free will becomes meaningless. In education, the teacher is the behavioral engineer, the one who structures the environment for the students.

The roots of this perspective are philosophic realism that dates back as far as Aristotle, who relied on the senses and reason to develop laws of nature to explain the world. For the realist, the world is to be known through laws that explain experience. Once laws are known, the world can be understood through reason. This approach was reasserted in the Nineteenth Century as positivism, primarily through the work of Auguste Comte. Comte insisted that a scientific view of the world must rely on observable and measurable facts. Pavlov, Watson and Skinner used this perspective in their work. Figure 2.6 emphasizes the observational nature of behaviorism and the rejection of explanations that account for behavior in terms of feelings or inner causes, and like other maps in this section, was based on a section of Knight's book (1998).

Skinner rejected appeal to feelings or consciousness to explain human behavior, since these explanations were neither observable nor scientific. The inner workings of the mind were a "black box", therefore, impenetrable and not to be used in the science of psychology as he wanted to develop it.

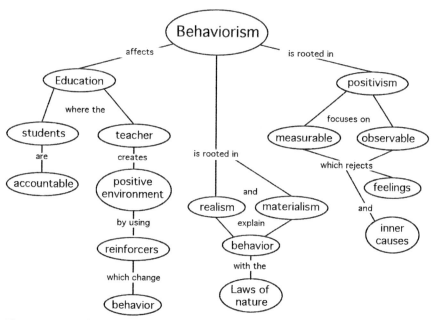

Figure 2.6. Student concept map for behaviorism.

This approach to psychology is consistent with a view called materialism. Materialism is consistent with philosophical realism, in that it stresses the importance of laws of matter and motion, especially the belief that for every effect there is a cause that lies outside the object. For Skinner, psychology should be intent on finding laws of behavior and learning. His work with rats and pigeons in the controlled environment of his Skinner box led to what he seemed to claim were laws of learning, as he developed elaborate mathematical models of reinforcement schedules that accounted for animals' behavior. His aim was to determine causes, external to the animal, and to disclaim inner feelings or consciousness as causes for behavior.

The behaviorist perspective can be summarized in several principles. Consistent with realism, as conceived by Aristotle, man is an animal. The behaviorists claim this to mean that if laws of learning for less complex animals were discovered, these laws would apply to human beings. Consequently, when the laws are discovered, educators should apply these laws of reinforcement to control the environmental factors in school. Students' behavior should be controlled by appropriate reinforcement schedules. For Skinner, the best schedules were those that involved positive reinforcement, and avoided attempts to punish students. Punishment was unpredictable and often led to rebellion. The most effective methods were to identify the appropriate outcome, remove any interference that might complicate the learning situation, select reinforcers that would shape behavior, implement the schedule until the target behavior was achieved, then assess the results and plan for future goals (Knight 1998).

This approach manifested itself in development of teaching machines, programmed learning, and behavioral objectives. As Knight says, behavioral techniques are valued for their "efficiency, economy, precision, and objectivity" (1998, 131). For these reasons, many advocates for "accountability" in schools favor this perspective. Their concern is about measurable outcomes, what students will know and be able to do.

Progressivism

This movement was part of a worldview that entered into politics of the late Nineteenth and early Twentieth Century in the United States. Progressivism linked to political activism through people like Robert La Follette and Woodrow Wilson. The aim was to make changes in America that would improve the social welfare of citizens being adversely affected by increased industrialization and urbanization. Progressive reformers saw education as a vehicle for social change.

Progressivism was a reaction against traditional education that seemed to impose learning in an authoritarian manner. Most progressive educators objected to the authoritarian teacher, emphasis on passive textbook learning and memorization, the isolation of students in classrooms, without outside contact or democratic participation, and reliance on harsh forms of discipline. Influence from the past, through the romantic notions of the French philosopher Jean Jacques Rousseau, about the inherent goodness of children and the adverse, corrupting influence of society caught the attention of educators like John Dewey. Dewey, born in 1859 in Burlington, Vermont, grew up believing in the ideas of small town democracy and developed a pragmatic view of learning. He pursued his interests in education as a school teacher in Pennsylvania; later, after receiving his doctorate from Johns Hopkins, as a professor at the University of Chicago, he established a laboratory school in 1896 to test his ideas.

Also, Sigmund Freud's work about the psychology of human beings influenced progressive ideas. Educators took Freud's work as a rationale to allow children more free expression. The belief was that more free expression would allow for healthier personal development. Figure 2.7 summarizes the history and aims of progressivism in the classroom.

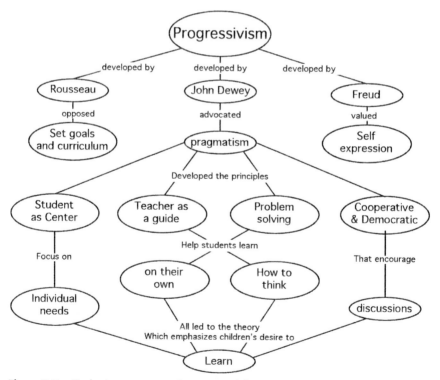

Figure 2.7. Student concept map for progressivism.

Rousseau's ideas expressed in his novel *Emile*—elaborating his romantic notions concerning educating—were used as arguments to allow more free expression by children. Many educators saw traditional adult attitudes as constraining the natural development of children. But, as Knight indicates, the "excesses of child-centered progressives were more in harmony with the thought of Rousseau and Freud than with that of Dewey, even though Dewey has generally received the blame by the many critics of progressive education" (1998, 97). Dewey's pragmatism and progressivism emphasized reflective thinking about knowledge and experience to guide teachers in the classroom.

Through the influence of many educators at Columbia University, especially William Kilpatrick and George Counts, progressive education influenced education theory and practice from the 1920s through the 1950s. On the positive side, progressive educators tended to share the following principles to define educating. They believed that the child is active and inquisitive. The aim of the curriculum should be to engage this natural interest. The teacher should take this interest and develop a learning environment that enhances the purpose of each child.

As much as possible, the child should be actively engaged in learning, using a problem solving approach. Generally, for Dewey, problem solving involved five steps: 1) a felt problem, one that genuinely puzzles the learner, 2) an assessment of why something is problematic. The aim is to offer 3) a hypothesis to solve the problem, 4) to anticipate probable outcomes of various hypotheses, and 5) to test the hypotheses and evaluate the outcomes, in order to reconsider the entire problem, or move on to new problems (1938). This requires active learning, and a teacher who is able to guide students through the various steps of the pragmatic method.

Teachers establish the learning environment. They guide students in various projects and discoveries, relying in part on the child's natural curiosity. This allows the child to explore the world from the classroom, in other words, "the school is a microcosm of the larger society" (Knight 1998, 100). How students learn in school should reflect the process of learning in the world outside the school. People are interested in all kinds of things, and learning outside of school follows the problem solving method that should guide learning in school. And because the society is democratic by design, for progressives, schools should reflect this fact. Schools need to mirror the social order. Schools need to develop democratically minded citizens who know how to cooperate with each other. The following section further elaborates upon Dewey's views about educating, ideas key to authentic educating.

Dewey's Theory of Experience

This chapter outlines six of the most common philosophic perspectives in education—views that are identified in the Educational Philosophy Inventory—to give you a better understanding of those with which you agree, and those with which you do not. But Dewey's and Gowin's theories about educating are further elaborated to show their connection to authentic educating. Dewey's view emphasized the importance of education in a process to develop a fully integrated personality (Dewey 1938).

For Dewey, the fully integrated personality is an aim in the process of growth. The fully integrated personality balances the ability to solve problems that is a product of developing the ability to think critically, with commitment to democratic principles, such as fairness and equality, as the individual finds a place in the larger society. Dewey believed that as the individual develops habits of thinking to understand past experience and grows toward implementing habits that emphasize the importance of democratic ideals, one grows toward a fully integrated personality. Self-educating is central to developing a fully integrated personality capable of authentic relationships with others.

The key concepts of Dewey's theory of experience are shown in a concept map below (Figure 2.8). This heuristic tool constructs the network of meaning among concepts in a hierarchical structure, from most general concept at the top to the most specific concept at the bottom. The concept map summarizes ideas from chapter three of *Experience and Education* (1938) that describe an American philosophic perspective called progressive education. Dewey's theory entails the principles of continuity, habit, and interaction. The principle of continuity suggests that previous experiences affect later experiences. Therefore, habit is affected by previous experiences and affects the quality of subsequent experience. Habits are attitudes that blend thinking and feeling. For Dewey, habits were more complex than a fixed way of doing things. Habits covered basic sensitivities, but also the ways people responded to new challenges. Therefore, habits were open to change through interaction in the process of growth. The principle of interaction stressed internal and external conditions that form a particular situation.

Dewey emphasized the importance of growth, which aims toward enhancement of intellectual and emotional powers, within the context of democratic ideals of equality contained in the Documents of Freedom and Obligation, which also identify a person's obligations in society. He believed that democracy is the best of all social institutions because it promotes the best quality of human experience. Fundamental to democracy is freedom, which allows the individual to contribute to the group that has commitment

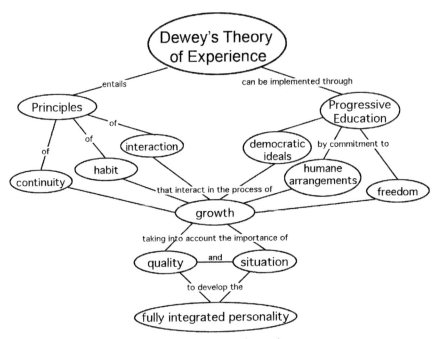

Figure 2.8. Concept map for Dewey's theory of experience.

to humane arrangements, not autocratic and harsh arrangements. Dewey emphasized that the three principles of experience: continuity, habit, and interaction offer criteria by which to judge democratic ideals and humane arrangements as superior to all other.

Dewey objected to traditional education that emphasized external conditions, like subject matter or harsh authority, to the exclusion of the internal conditions such as interest, ability, or sophistication. On the opposite extreme, but equally misguided, was education that indulged students' internal interests without aims toward a fully integrated personality—according to Dewey this made people "scatter-brained" (1938, 26).

For Dewey, education of quality accounts for internal and external interaction to create the proper situation. The example Dewey offered was a wise parent who attended to a baby's needs for food, sleep, etc. by applying knowledge about how children grow physically and mentally. By taking responsibility for the child's internal needs and controlling the external environment, the wise parent creates an interactive situation that leads toward the child's growth. For example, a parent puts the child in a crib for rest when the child may want to continue to play, or snatches the child from near a fire, or regulates the feeding schedule, always with concern for the child's growth.

Habits are generated in the situation in which the parent is concerned about the continuity of the child's experience. When a parent wants the child to grow toward a fully integrated personality, internal and external conditions are balanced. The long-term goal is toward democratic arrangements as the child matures, and parent and child move toward greater exercise of intelligence to solve problems that integrate successive experiences (Dewey 1938). The goal is to develop an integrated personality, so the child may grow to an adult who knows how to solve problems and uses these abilities to become a productive member of a democratic society.

The process is similar for educators. The aim toward developing the fully integrated personality is key. Habits are to be developed by taking into account students' previous experiences and internal conditions to move them toward growth within the objective conditions of the classroom. As Dewey indicated, the external objective conditions include what the teacher does and says (including tone of voice), what equipment, materials, books, and apparatus are used, or games played in the classroom, or homework given. The teacher must balance the principles of continuity, habit and interaction with commitment to democratic ideals, humane arrangements and freedom to create quality situations that lead toward the fully integrated personality.

Applying this theoretical approach in education—movement toward democratic ideals and human arrangements—entails taking into account each student's previous experiences and internal conditions. This implies acknowledging the importance of cultural experience to create worthwhile educational experience. Dewey indicated a problem with traditional education was the emphasis on the external conditions, and not enough emphasis on the power and purpose of the students being taught. But he was equally critical of the opposite extreme, of indulging students' interests at the moment, without a view about future growth, as misguided education.

Growth occurs when individuals learn to solve problems that connect experiences from the past with those of the future, in ways that generate new habits. For Dewey, education should empower people to solve problems. Education should emphasize the importance of democratic ideals, commitment to humane arrangements and freedom interacting in this process of growth toward a fully integrated personality. The fully integrated person takes from previous experiences to enhance future experiences, but also participates in various associations like family and professional life. Dewey saw these associations as part of membership in a democratic society, whose purpose is to educate members of society to their fullest potential. The aim of democratic education is to develop individuals who share a common spirit and common aims (Campbell 1995). Dewey's theory is part of the philosophic foundation used to construct authentic educating.

Existentialism

Existentialism emphasizes the individual's search for meaning. In this way, it is neither a systematic philosophy, nor one enamored with the intellect. The roots are scattered in various parts of Europe in the late Nineteenth and early Twentieth Century. Many people give the Danish writer Soren Kierkegaard (1813-1855) credit as the first existentialist—a conflicted and tormented man who seemed at times to advocate Christianity and at other times wallow in despair. But for most Christian existentialists, they emphasize personal meaning, and their relationship with God, in a way that makes Christianity not a social event confined to Sunday, but a way of life that finds meaning in Christ-like living. Other Christian existentialists, such as the Catholic theologian Gabriel Marcel (1887-1973) or the Protestant theologian Paul Tillich (1886-1965) emphasized the importance of Christians living the faith of their religion in daily life.

At the opposite extreme, philosophers like Friedrich Nietzsche (1844-1900) railed against Christianity, and declared the death of God. For Nietzsche, who postulated a "superman" who would go *Beyond Good and Evil*, Christianity elicited a herd morality that was the enemy of individuality and man's will to power. It is this side of existentialism, the atheistic, that seems to have gotten more media attention, and branded existentialism as a philosophy of nihilism and despair. Advocates like the French philosopher Jean Paul Sartre (1905-1980) and Albert Camus (1913-1960) were accused of pessimism. Their denial of God and their bleak worldview were highly criticized. But, existentialists often could not agree among themselves what existentialism consisted of, and one of the humorous hallmarks of existentialists was denying that they were existentialists. Heidegger, the German philosopher denied being an existentialist if Sartre and Camus were considered existentialists, and vice versa.

Although existentialism does not lead to a systematic philosophy, there do appear to be common themes among those identified as existentialists. One of the key aspects is the individual's subjective responsibility. The purpose of life, for the existentialists, is to define oneself. For Sartre, who claimed the key principle of existentialism to be "existence precedes essence," (Ayer and O'Grady 1992, 397) this translates to individual responsibility for choices that define existence and create one's essence through personal action. The following map summarizes key concepts of existentialism (Figure 2.9).

Since individuals define themselves through choices, truth becomes dependent upon the choices one makes. So truth is what one chooses. Translated into epistemology—the study of knowledge—truth becomes subjective, contingent on personal choice. In this way, as one chooses, one defines what values to live by, and so axiology, the study of values, becomes subjective

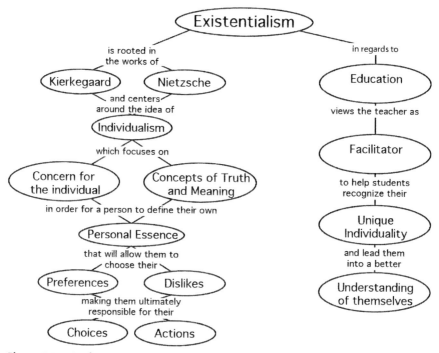

Figure 2.9. Student concept map for existentialism in education.

also. In summary then, the philosophic structure of existentialism rests heavily on the subjective individual.

In Sartre's case his claim that "existence precedes essence" (Ayer and O'Grady 1992, 397) manifest into the pessimistic statement "Hell is other people" in his play *No Exit* (404), and a worldview that saw all relationships as sado-masochistic. For him, it also led at times to embracing Communism. In Heidegger's case, this subjective worldview led him to become a Nazi sympathizer while he was teaching at Freiburg University during Hitler's reign in Germany. However, for Camus, it led to the French resistance in Paris during World War II and an editorial role at *Combat*, an anti-Nazi magazine. Clearly, each of the philosophers took different approaches to individual subjectivity and responsibility. But each of them claimed personal responsibility to be a matter of "authenticity." The concept of "authenticity" arises in both theistic and atheistic existentialism. But of these three atheistic philosophers, only Camus seems to have a view that allowed for human solidarity in ways untainted by totalitarian political movements. However, to advocate existentialism in American schools, neither Sartre's nor Heidegger's approach are appropriate. Only Camus, who defined himself through rebellion against all forms of oppression, could be considered a sympathetic advocate.

Existentialist ideas in the classroom emphasize the importance of the individual. Students should be allowed freedom to make choices. The curriculum should be open ended. Most existentialists would agree that children need to learn basic skills, but the methodology cannot be tedious or be confined to meaningless drills. The emphasis should always be on the personal meaning of the educational experience. The aim is to have students learn to take responsibility as they define themselves through personal choices. The following section describes Gowin's theory of educating, a theory which emphasizes the importance of personal meaning as a key concept in educating, and therefore, he described as an existential theory.

Gowin's Theory of Educating

The theory D. Bob Gowin described in his book *Educating* (1981) is consistent with an existential philosophic perspective because it emphasizes the importance of "meaning" in education, and emphasizes events of educating that result from deliberate intervention in people's lives with meaningful materials. Similar to Dewey, Gowin was concerned to develop habits that lead toward growth. In educating, the use of excellent materials is important in the context of four commonplaces of education: teaching, learning, curriculum, and governance.

With a theory of educating to guide one's practice, it is possible to be clear about intentions and outcomes. For Gowin, educating aims at changing the meaning of students' experience. The goal is to help students learn actively so that they are eventually able to learn on their own. When thinking about educating this way, one realizes that what people talk about *is* the meaning of their experience; it is what having a voice is about.

Gowin's theory of educating fits into an existential philosophic perspective. As the following map shows, he emphasizes the importance of personal meaning in education and aims at integrating thinking, feeling, and acting to achieve self-educating (Figure 2.10; from Gowin 1981, 94).

He considered educating as an active process that assumes people can change. For Gowin, educating is an eventful process that presupposes the possibility of change and which leads to a change in the meaning of experience. For example, an educative event occurs when a music teacher deliberately intervenes by writing suggestions on a music score for a young student to show particular skills necessary to perform a piece. Gowin, like Dewey, was concerned about changing habits—that he called habitual dispositions—that are a person's usual ways of approaching a situation. In the music example, the teacher's intervention is directed to change the student's habitual dispositions. The change occurs when the student is able to integrate thinking

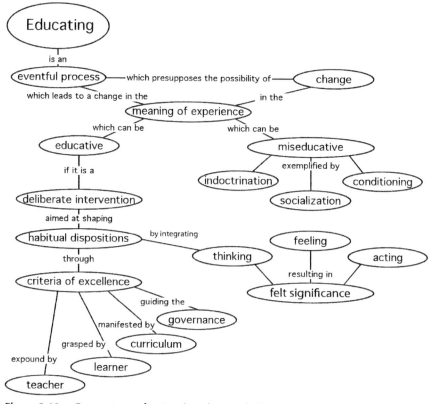

Figure 2.10. Concept map for Gowin's theory of education.

about the notes and suggestions on the score, feeling about the way to play the instrument, and acting to produce an improved piece. When thinking, feeling and acting integrate, the results are felt significance, an intellectual and emotional appreciation for the improvements generated by learning. In educating, habitual dispositions change in relationship to criteria of excellence that are established through interaction with the four commonplaces of the teacher, learner, curriculum and governance, usually called administration.

Gowin claimed "Teaching is the achievement of shared meaning in the context of educating" (1981, 62). As an authority, the teacher has information to convey to a student. The teacher works to make the material understandable to the student, for example, the teacher shares a musical score with written suggestions on it that the student needs to grasp. The teacher, in turn, determines if the student correctly understands the suggestions. This interaction, when successful, leads to a change in the meaning of the student's experience. When the student uses the suggestions, it is possible for learning to occur.

Learning occurs when the learner grasps meanings the teacher shares and actively reorganizes the suggestions, affecting habits and improving performance. Gowin defined learning as the "active reorganization of an existing pattern of meaning" (1981, 124). Learning is a deliberate act; the learner reorganizes new meanings with old meanings to construct new patterns, to see more connections among the things one knows. For Gowin, one of the most important things in education is what the learner claims to know. This is the starting point for learning. Also significant in education, is that feelings accompany learning. As one grasps meanings, one feels the significance of what one learns, giving it a sense of value.

To facilitate meaningful learning, one of the heuristic tools that Gowin and Novak (1984) developed was the concept map—a hierarchical visual construction of the relationships among key concepts—used throughout this book. The concept map externalizes thinking to show relationships among concepts, thus, a concept map gives powerful insight into what a student understands and the connections a student makes among concepts. How to construct maps is described in the next chapter.

The curriculum in the music example is the musical score with the teacher's suggestions written on it. Generally, curriculum is a set of materials selected by the teacher that are key to a particular subject. The curriculum is the knowledge taught, the subject matter of educative events. It is the source for teaching, and when assessed, educative materials "must pass two major tests: one comes from the standards of the field from which the work originates and the other comes from standards of education" (Gowin 1981, 113). Events in educating require that teachers expound a curriculum constructed with a view toward the criteria of excellence in the field. Guided by humane arrangements in the classroom, learners grasp the curriculum, with the aim of changing the meaning of their experience. Gowin's definition is that "a curriculum is a logically connected set of conceptually and pedagogically analyzed knowledge and value claims" (1981, 109).

To conceptually analyze a curriculum, Gowin suggests the use of the Vee (to be described in Chapter 4). The Vee is a heuristic tool to assess the key questions, concepts, principles and theories contained in the curriculum. A Vee can be used to evaluate what Gowin calls the criteria of excellence, the criteria that justify particular curriculum as an example of excellent content within a particular discipline. The Vee can be used to assess selection of a particular literary work, or musical piece, or research study in the sciences. To pedagogically analyze curriculum means to assess it for how to teach it, what students are to learn, and how their learning is to be evaluated.

Teaching, learning and curriculum are harmonized by governance, which controls the events in educating. In a democratic society, the major concern is for justice, a sense of fairness for the participants because the aim is to improve the quality of educating. Gowin contrasts the concern for social justice in educative events with miseducative approaches such as indoctrination, socialization and conditioning.

Indoctrination occurs when people are taught what to believe without evidence for belief. Socialization attributes roles and characteristics to people without opportunities for alternative choices and, therefore, results in stereotypes, such as girls should be nurses and boys should be doctors. In conditioning, choice disappears and behavior is controlled externally, such as when animals are trained to perform for food rewards. For Gowin educative events are of different quality and, therefore, are more complex, because they depend on criteria of excellence in a discipline and their meaning is established through reason and evidence.

The aim of educating is to help students control their own powers and abilities, as they move toward the goal of becoming self-educators, which means they are able to learn on their own. Self-educating begins after one achieves a broad understanding of key concepts in a particular subject matter, and one is able to evaluate that knowledge. As one integrates new meanings into old and reorganizes meanings, knowledge expands. One is better able to judge knowledge by criteria of excellence in a field, and becomes an authority (Gowin 1981).

Perennialism

As an educational philosophy, perennialism was a reaction against progressivism in the 1930s. Perennialists believed that the progressive strategies in schools were abandoning the intellectual values that form a liberal education. Perennialists believed that emphasis on the child as center of the curriculum and focus on activity departed from attending to the importance of the rational mind. Liberal education, as far back as Plato and Aristotle centered on developing reason. For the perennialist, that tradition should be maintained, and liberal education should be the center of curriculum. In Plato's *Republic*, education was aimed at development of reason, and for Aristotle, man was a rational animal; therefore, the key to education was development of reasoning ability.

Two of the most influential advocates for perennialism were Robert Maynard Hutchins (1899-1977) and Mortimer J. Adler (1902-2002), both from the University of Chicago. In the 1930s, Hutchins was president of the university and Adler was a prominent member of the philosophy department. Together they developed a series of books called *Great Books of the Western World*, which they believed represented the collected wisdom of Western

civilization, as far back as the Greeks (Knight, 1998). They promoted the use
of these books as a basis for a liberal arts education. Perennialists emphasize
education that focuses the rational mind on the great works to show that
knowledge is universal and permanent.

Adler continued as a major influence in perennialist education, especially
through establishment of the Institute for Philosophical Research and development of a common curriculum for public schooling called the Paideia Pro-
posal. He emphasized that quality education in public schools should rest on a
similar foundation for all students, "at the basic level, giving all the young the
same kind of schooling, whether or not they are college bound" (Noll 1999,
18). This is consistent with Hutchins' claims, almost fifty years earlier, that
"Education implies teaching. Teaching implies knowledge. Knowledge is
truth. Truth is everywhere the same. Hence education should be everywhere
the same" (Knight 1998, 110).

Allan Bloom promoted the perennialist viewpoint in his best seller *The
Closing of the American Mind* (1987). Bloom was highly critical of the
way curriculum, even at America's finest universities, was being diluted by
courses without academic rigor. For him, what many universities offered as a
liberal arts education was not worthy of being called education. Bloom's criticism seemed to echo Hutchins' warning that "the death of democracy is not
likely to be an assassination from ambush. It will be a slow extinction from
apathy, indifference, and undernourishment" (Kaplan 1992, 702). The following student map identifies Hutchins and Adler as key to perennialism and
shows their focus on the importance of developing the rational mind through
exposure to great works (Figure 2.11).

For perennialists, the function of the school is to educate the intellect.
"Education deals with the development of the intellectual powers of men.
Their moral and spiritual powers are the sphere of the family and the church"
(Noll 1999, 12). The school, family and church must work in harmony for
Hutchins. But the school is neither a place for moral or vocational training.
School is not a place to adjust students to society, but to teach them eternal
truths handed down in the "Great Books."

With the collective wisdom of the West as the key to curriculum, and training of the rational mind as the goal, it is subject matter that is central to educating, not the child's interests. Educating disciplines the child's mind. "Difficult mental exercises, including reading, writing, drill, rote memory, and
computation, are significant in training and disciplining the intellect" (Noll
1999, 111). Consequently, the methods tend to focus on "didactic instruction, lectures and responses, coaching, exercises, and supervised practice in
the operations of reading, writing, speaking, listening, calculating, problem-

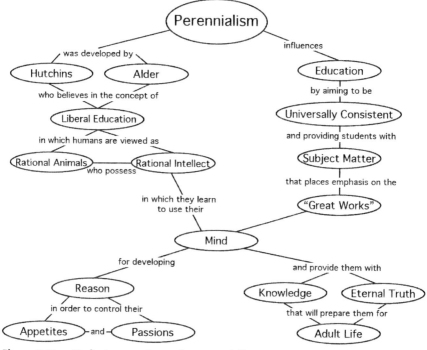

Figure 2.11. Student concept map for perennialism.

solving, observing, measuring, estimating" (Morrison 2000, 430). All this is so that schools will be places that students are prepared for life, after their rational minds have been developed and trained appropriately.

Reconstructionism

If you strongly agreed with the claim in statement 12 of the Inventory that, "Schools should lead society toward radical social change" you probably sympathize with the reconstructionists. In 1932, George Counts (1889–1974)—a student of Dewey—published his influential book *Dare the Schools Build a New Social Order?* In it he "laid out the basic tenets of reconstructionism, including developing a new social foundation for society and educating students to be agents of social change" (Morrison 2000, 438). The movement was based on Dewey's pragmatic philosophy and progressive educational ideas. The word itself can be tied to Dewey's influential book *Democracy and Education* and his: "technical definition of education: It is that reconstruction or reorganization of experience which adds to the meaning of experience, and which increases ability to direct the course of subsequent experience" (1916, 76).

This perspective developed during a critical period of social turmoil and worldwide economic depression. Counts encouraged educators to be active in social reform through the schools. Theodore Brameld (1904-1987) advocated this approach during the 1950s and 60s.

The basic principles of this perspective were that civilization is in crisis, with totalitarian regimes and democracy in conflict. The economic social order of the 1930s was at best precarious, and the political order of the Cold War potentially catastrophic. Schools could not remain in the shadows of these social needs, content to transmit traditional values. Schools needed to be catalysts of change. Nothing less than a new world social order needed to be constructed, and students needed to learn problem-solving skills to become part of it.

If my elementary school experience in the Fifties can be considered typical, discussions about and field trips to the United Nations were supposed to alert us kids that the problems were real—although at times terrifying, especially the threat of nuclear annihilation that forced drills to practice hiding under our desks—but solvable in some vague yet undiscovered way among people of good will. The task of schools, teachers and students was to find solutions on a global level—much like Jonas Salk's hard work led to the discovery of a vaccine to combat polio worldwide and the reason a new junior high school in our town was named in his honor. For reconstructionists, the task was to prepare students to become leaders in the future for the world to continue to exist at all.

The social philosophy of reconstructionists and their teaching methods were based on democratic principles. "Reconstructionists, like those in other branches of the progressive movement, are unified in their view of democracy as the best political system" (Knight, 1998, 121). Therefore, as much as possible, democratic procedures needed to be used in the classroom.

Other recent educators seem to fit this reconstructionist perspective. James Banks, a major voice in multicultural education (1992), advocates schools as the place to make changes in peoples' attitudes toward different cultures in America. Banks outlines several levels of multicultural education in the schools, but emphasizes the importance of developing critical thinking skills. His aim is to make better students and better citizens. Henry Giroux's *Postmodernism, Feminism, and Cultural Politics* (1991) is a collection of essays from the "critical pedagogy" perspective, a movement in education that uses postmodern and feminist ideas in the classroom, with the aim to reconstruct society. Clearly, educators advocating radical change in schools continue to raise their voices (Figure 2.12).

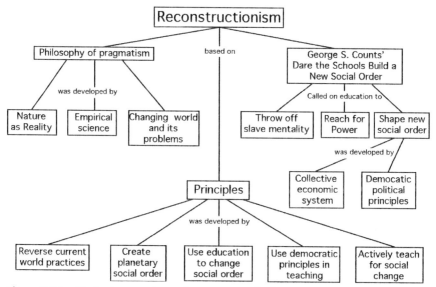

Figure 2.12. Student concept map for reconstructionism.

FINAL THOUGHTS ABOUT DEVELOPING
A PHILOSOPHY OF EDUCATION

Over the years of standardizing the Educational Philosophy Inventory, I have worked with Stetson graduate students to survey hundreds of undergraduate and graduate students and teachers in the field (Griffis 1998; King 2000; Dailey 2002). The results of our research suggest that a majority of students planning to become teachers and teachers in the schools tend toward the philosophic perspectives of progressivism and existentialism (Griffis 1998; Dailey 2002). However, the present educational environment seems inclined toward essentialism, such that, the longer one stays, the more likely one is to be an essentialist (Dailey 2002).

Our research indicates that many teachers leave the field after a few years, and students aspiring toward education change their majors, in part, from their field experience in public schools that indicates to them that public school teaching may not satisfy their philosophic perspectives about education. The results are clear at the state and national level, that there are not sufficient teachers being drawn into the field or remaining in the schools; consequently, the teacher shortage remains critical. Teachers cite various reasons for leaving teaching, such as overcrowded classrooms, disruptive students, lack of administrative support, low pay, and heightened emphasis on prescribed curriculum and pervasive standardized testing (King 2000).

King's study of Florida legislators and approximately three hundred undergraduate students enrolled in education courses in central Florida colleges indicates there are an overwhelming number of students inclined toward progressive and existential perspectives, and a significant number advocating a reconstructionist perspective—a viewpoint that advocates schools should become a more radical force for social change. However, the Florida legislators surveyed—most of whom failed to respond to the survey—seemed to advocate essentialist views and, given continued insistence upon standardized testing and prescribed curriculum as the key means to assess school performance, they are *de facto* inclined toward essentialism. Consequently, the Griffis (1998) King (2000) and Dailey (2002) studies indicate that the current school climate is less likely to attract sufficient teachers for the public school needs. The schools do not have enough teachers, but the essentialist environment seems unlikely to attract people inclined to teach for progressive and existential motives.

Authentic educating, which relies on progressive and existential perspectives, is likely to appeal to aspiring teachers and teachers in the field, but, unfortunately, many are skeptical or even cynical about how it can fit into the current educational climate. Obviously, a theory that advocates what the majority of teachers believe—about the student as focus of education and the content as meaningful to the student—would be more appealing if it could address the essentialist agenda driving the schools. I agree, and several Stetson graduate students have done or are doing research of this sort, with encouraging results. However, I believe the most beneficial approach would be a search for common ground among the essentialists, primarily legislators who control the money and the policies, and teachers, motivated by progressive and existential perspectives.

REVIEW AND REFLECT

Phase I: The dialogue process is essential to ensure that students are aware of the oral and written arguments that are prevalent in current educating.

1. Divide the class into teams of three for the purpose of conducting a debate on the top five issues raised about American education.
2. The topic for discussion can be selected by a simple drawing from a hat. Once the teams have the topic, then they should prepare for the debate.
3. The debate should be thirty minutes on each issue, which includes audience questions and feedback from the instructor.

4. Culminate the debate process with an open discussion about the issues discussed.

Phase II: Reflective Journal Writing

1. Write about your perceptions, feelings and concerns with current education. The instructor should respond to students' work to make the process interactive.

For Further Study:

1. Select any of the concept maps in this chapter and write a paragraph about how the key concepts would affect the way you teach your subject.
2. Imagine that you are preparing a lesson in your field. Construct a concept map that identifies seven to nine concepts that you want to teach. Organize the map so that the major concept is at the top and related concepts are in hierarchical order with connecting words to show relationships among concepts.
3. Remember an experience with teachers of a philosophic perspective different from your own, write a paragraph about how the experience taught you something about yourself.
4. List ten things about your educational philosophy that you believe should be incorporated in current education practices and explain why.

Chapter Three

How to Use Concept Maps

Concept maps show relationships among key concepts in any field. The learning Vee described in the next chapter shows how knowledge is constructed. These two heuristics used together are powerful tools to help students move toward high level thinking. To begin this chapter, I summarize how to construct and assess concept maps, then give examples of student maps to summarize plots of several novels. In subsequent chapters, I show how students use concept maps as one of the tools to consider issues of authenticity in their own lives.

HOW TO CONSTRUCT A CONCEPT MAP

The concept map (Figure 3.1) was drawn by a first grader, from a list of concepts about animals (Novak and Gowin 1984, 177).

The steps to construct a concept map are:

First make a list of the words to be mapped. In the map below, the key concepts are: animals, mammals, reptiles, dogs, cats, snakes, lizards, fur, scales.

Second, put the most general concept at the top of the map. In this science lesson, students considered categories of animals, then examples that fit the categories, and finally, characteristics.

Third, put concepts of equal importance on the same horizontal. From the list for this example, after animals, the next two concepts of equal importance and specificity are mammals and reptiles. They are the two major categories into which animals are divided for this map.

Fourth, place words of equal importance and specificity on the same horizontal: dogs, cats, snakes, lizards. These are examples that fit the two categories.

concepts   concept mapping   name

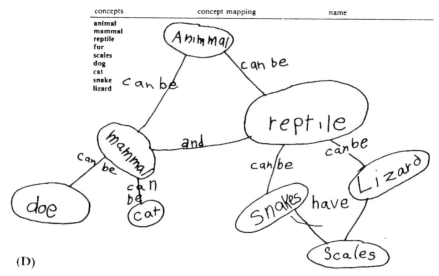

animal
mammal
reptile
fur
scales
dog
cat
snake
lizard

(D)

Figure 3.1. First grader's concept map about animals.

Fifth, continue the placement of words on appropriate horizontals until all words are used. As mammals, dogs and cats share the characteristic of fur. Reptiles such as snakes and lizards share the characteristic of scales.

Sixth, connect related key concepts with lines and connecting words that make clear statements about the relationship between key concepts. Words like "can be" and "have" show clear relationships. They make connections between the concepts by stating propositions.

A concept map should make sense to the one who constructs it, and also show connections among concepts in a network of meaning that can be read by others. A concept map gives a visual picture in a concise organized way.

THE VALUE OF CONCEPT MAPS

The value of concept maps is that they require one to organize key concepts and construct meaningful relationships among them. When constructing concept maps from texts or a piece of writing, students need to read the material and make judgments about which concepts are central to the meaning of the text. By first selecting the central concepts, students go beyond a superficial read. Extracting concepts requires identifying their importance in context, then listing them. The next, more difficult task is to create a hierarchy by deciding the relative importance of the concepts and a series of meaningful relationships among them. This requires high-level thinking: the ability to synthesize the concepts and evaluate how the meanings relate to each other.

In the above map, the student used two categories: mammals and reptiles, to further identify animals. This distinction allows the student to further clarify the meaning of animals (although he misspelled it) by giving examples of animals that fit into each of the two categories. This entails knowing which animals fit into the category, and then requires understanding of particular characteristics of these examples, which further clarifies the concepts. For example, this first grade student identified dogs and cats as mammals, and knows that a characteristic of mammals is that they have fur.

A valuable benefit of concept maps is that they encourage students to work from low to high levels of thinking, i.e. they must first identify key concepts, then organize them into a meaningful network. The skills involved encompass the levels of thinking that Bloom identified in his *Taxonomy of Educational Objectives* (1956).

Bloom's six levels are: starting at the lowest level, of recall, naming concepts that he called *knowledge*. *Comprehension* is the ability to explain concepts in one's own words; *application* entails using concepts in context to solve problems; *analysis* requires being able to assess complex ideas into their simpler parts; *synthesis* is the ability to take simple ideas and organize them into a new order; and, finally, the highest level, *evaluation* is the ability to make judgments about the usefulness or value of ideas to solve problems.

When one extracts concepts to organize into a concept map, these various levels of thinking come into play. At first the map maker must organize the concepts, which usually requires revising the map several times to fit the concepts together in a meaningful way and to defend the map for the concepts under consideration. As Novak and Gowin acknowledge in a footnote (1984, 23), there is criticism of Bloom's conceptual framework, but teachers tend to agree with Bloom's claim that there are various levels of thinking. The challenge is to get students to higher levels of thinking. Over the years, I have found concept mapping to be an excellent tool to involve students in this range of thinking.

I remember back in the Sixties, when I was a new junior high school science teacher, Bloom's ideas were popular in our department. County administrators and teachers discussed planning curriculum to address each level of his taxonomy. The aim was to involve students in high level thinking through learning science actively, in the lab.

We had workshops to learn how to write learning objectives. Afterward, we were required to submit lesson plans in advance to our department chairman on triple sheets of NCR paper, outlining how we were to accomplish student learning in Bloom's cognitive, psychomotor and affective domains.

But my chairman reminded us that the county-wide standardized exam never went above the application level of thinking, nor did they test the psychomotor or affective domain.

While our science program was advertised as innovative and comprehensive, as a classroom teacher, I was told to make sure my students knew content to perform well on the county test. The message I got from our chairman was that attempts to develop higher-level thinking, manual skills, and moral attitudes may be noble, but was to be left for someone else—something I have been thinking about since, and which led me to develop authentic educating.

Critics claim the levels of Bloom's taxonomy are ambiguous. But even if they are accurate, *how* does a teacher get students to think at various levels? Also, since it is primarily a taxonomy, a means of classifying things, again, *how to* address cognitive, psychomotor and affective domains remained a puzzle. Mager's (1962) work, which became popular at the time emphasized techniques of writing behavioral objectives, but seemed to offer few tools to make things happen in the classroom.

What I like about Novak and Gowin's concept mapping heuristic tool is that it encourages one to think in various ways. By applying the strategies, one understands that as a learner or teacher, the goal is to make sense of concepts. As they wrote "Concept maps can foster cooperation between student and teacher (or child and school) in a battle in which the *monster* to be conquered is meaninglessness of information and victory is shared meaning" (1984, 23).

The purpose of concept mapping is to show relationships among concepts. The techniques can be learned by young children, as demonstrated in the previous example, and remain the same as students become more proficient and sophisticated throughout their education. Also, it tends to appeal to visual learners, which many students are. Whether drawn on paper or constructed using computer graphics, it involves both the mind and hands. This tends to make learning more fun, and tends to help students remember what they draw.

GRADING CONCEPT MAPS

Look at the following four examples, A-D, in Figure 3.2. They were constructed in a first-grade class. Decide which is clearly the weakest and why, and which is clearly the strongest, and why. As you consider each, remember that you are looking for a hierarchy, clear categories, examples, and characteristics of those examples within each category. The concepts should connect with each other in meaningful statements, and the map should make sense. See what you think.

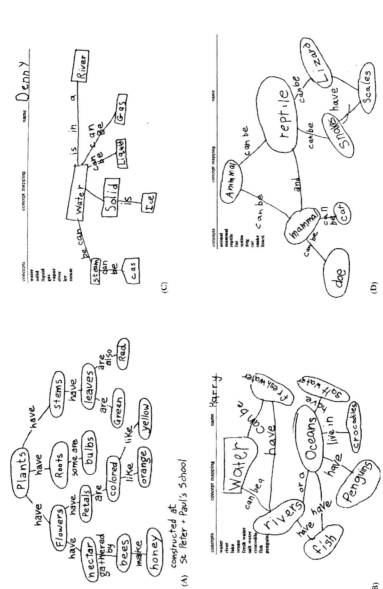

Figure 3.2. Sample first graders' concept maps.

These concept maps appear in the appendix of *Learning How to Learn* (1984, 176-177). The hand drawn examples give a feel for the first graders' psychomotor skills, and have added appeal for that reason, and because the drawings give other clues about the students. But when I give this problem— deciding among the weakest and strongest maps—to elementary through graduate students, there are interesting discussions. Harry's map about water (B) is identified as the weakest. Harry should identify water as fresh water and salt water and arrange the concepts accordingly.

The example I used at the beginning of this chapter—example D—has to do with concepts related to animals. To teach how to concept map, I usually have a blank transparency on the overhead projector or a projected computer image in PowerPoint to a large screen, then elicit responses from the group about concepts that first graders would use in science class to discuss animals. Often the suggestions begin with words like: large, small, friendly . . . But I suggest that group members think about animals like scientists.

After a few more suggestions like the previous ones, students offer words like dogs and cats . . . that I record on the transparency or computer screen. I filter the suggestions to make the list you see in D from the concepts randomly volunteered. I encourage students to think like first graders, but to name *scientific categories*. I usually get things like large and small, again. But I emphasize that we are in science . . . what *categories* might first graders name? Someone usually insists on furry. So I write down fur. Inevitably someone will say dinosaur. Someone will call out extinct . . . or Jurassic Park . . . or sauropod or Tyrannosaurus rex, or DNA cloned from amber . . . There will be various amounts of laughter, and other random thoughts, but someone usually volunteers the word *lizard* . . . That I record.

Often there is silence when I ask again if anyone can name large categories that first graders would use to classify animals. Somehow, someone usually comes up with *reptile*. Then another adds fish, or birds, or mammals, or amphibians. If there are biology majors in the group, I might hear vertebrates or invertebrates . . . or something like echinodermata. But then many in the group seem to believe that we are getting too scientific—unless, of course, there is a first grade teacher in the group, who offers testimony that corroborates the seeming tangent of the dinosaur discussion, with more sophisticated examples from the invertebrate world. Anyway, slowly, by asking questions, and listening selectively, then editing responses, I get the list of nine concepts in D within a few minutes of silence, some laughter then anxiety—when I ask each participant to construct a map from the list we generate, to compete with first graders.

I circulate around the room to watch their map construction. Occasionally, I repeat the directions: all nine key concepts are to be circled and appear in the map; the key concept *animal* is at the top; the finished map should have categories, examples then characteristics of those examples in a hierarchy; concepts of equal importance should appear at the same horizontal level in the map. I remind them to connect the concepts with lines, and to use connecting words to show the relationship between the concepts they have connected.

Most students finish within three to five minutes. Then I hand out a photocopy of maps A-D, and ask them to decide after discussion with a partner which is clearly the strongest, and which is clearly the weakest. We start by discussing the weakest. Maps B and C are most commonly chosen. Usually, most select B.

In Novak and Gowin's book, the name on the map is Harry. So I ask what weaknesses people see with Harry's work. Apart from Harry's lack of organization in the map, the biggest problem seems to be that Harry does not see a simple distinction between types of water. The suggestion is that if Harry divided water into *salt water* and *fresh water*, he could organize his map. Harry could benefit from Ken Strike's suggestion that "When in doubt make a distinction!" Concept maps are tools to help students make distinctions.

Then Harry would be able to give examples of *fresh water* as *lake* and *river* and *salt water* using *ocean*. Special cases like the Great Salt Lake in Utah or the brackish water where the Mississippi River meets the Gulf of Mexico offer interesting discussions. And quality and subtlety of discussions about maps depend upon the quality and subtlety of individuals in the group.

Although *fish* live in both *salt water* and *fresh water*, *crocodiles* and *penguins* live in *salt water*. How to handle this on a map leads to various possibilities. Another concern mentioned is that Harry makes several words that appear singular on the list plural in the map. But the somewhat poetic claim *"Oceans* live in *crocodiles"* gets mentioned often, and Harry does appear to be somewhat of a mystic, because his map drifts around the page.

The other map with difficulties is C. The name on this map in the Appendix (1984, 177) is Denny. The major problem students identify is that Denny doesn't seem to see that the list names the three states of matter and gives examples of each. Denny seems interested in the *river* being seen as important as *water*, and so puts them on the same horizontal level, not realizing that *river* works much better as an example of *liquid*. Also, he does not use the word *vapor*, or see the connections among *vapor, gas* and *steam*. He ends by using *gas* and *steam* separately on the map, and appears to spell this *vapor* form as *cas* and *gas*.

Maps A and D are selected as the strongest. Map A, which does not contain a list of words, is very neatly drawn as it appears in the Appendix (176). It has a significant amount of concepts in it, and students usually realize the teacher constructed it. It has three categories on the same horizontal: *flowers, roots,* and *stems.* Each of those concepts is clarified with an example. Often, students remark that it could be used for science discussions, or even become the groundwork for a language arts lesson. Some biology majors claim the map is confusing because the basic plant parts are *roots, stems* and *leaves,* and that *flowers* are merely specialized leaf adaptations that do not appear in all plants. Clearly, maps are open to interpretation, and how the map was generated, and for what purpose, enters into discussion of a finished piece. But, primarily, it is a tool for making meaning, and enthusiastic discussion of maps can lead to valuable learning.

Map D may have caught your attention because the word *doe* appears on it, although it doesn't appear on the list of words. On the hand drawn map, the letter "e" appears to be a classic example of the letter "g" reversed. This can lead to all sorts of discussions about appropriate interventions with the map maker, especially since the word *fur* is omitted. It is edifying to listen to the range of discussion around that difficulty, spanning from "leave it alone" to prescriptions for Ritalin!

By the end of discussion of these four maps, most students feel confident that they can match a first grader's expertise in map construction. Further, they believe they can see a distinction between a well-constructed map and a weak one. Map A is usually considered an A quality map. Map D tends to get graded as a B, because of the misspelling, letter reversal, and omission of the word *fur.* Both maps about water tend to be evaluated as poor work, because they lack clear distinctions, and supporting examples. But Harry's map seems clearly the weakest to almost all students because it lacks simple distinctions and organization.

Most students give themselves at least a C for their own work concept mapping the list of animals, and generally, their maps are quite good. Soon after, elementary through graduate students are able to construct computer generated concept maps to summarize novels they read or select to perform as one-act plays. Undergraduate and graduate students concept map and Vee diagram articles from Noll's (1999) *Taking Sides: Clashing Views on Controversial Educational Issues* for panel discussions. Their maps, photocopied for distribution, and shown as PowerPoint presentations are discussed after the play performance and as part of a panel discussion about the articles. In a required senior research course for the College of Arts and Sciences, I have education majors use concept maps to help clarify and drive their projects, and for their presentation to students and faculty. I agree with Novak and Gowin (1984) that concept mapping can be a valuable tool to improve and evaluate educational research. Undergraduate and graduate students used the maps that appeared in Chapter 2 to summarize educational philosophies for class presentations about philosophic perspectives in Knight's *Issues and*

Alternatives in Educational Philosophy (1998), and for various projects that they conduct with their own students in the schools.

REFINING AND SCORING CONCEPT MAPS

Novak and Gowin devote several pages (1984, 24-34) in their book to suggest ways to introduce various age students to concept mapping. They emphasize the importance for learners to grasp that we think with concepts. Concepts name things, like table and chair, and so, we can picture them in our mind. Events, like running and jumping are also concepts and can be pictured. We teach about concepts when we define them, give attributes and examples then make distinctions between them. As learners grasp that concepts convey meaning and can be pictured, it helps them to see the power of maps. Maps can externalize our thinking, and show others how we connect concepts into meaningful patterns.

How we connect concepts is by using *linking words*, such as: is, are, can be. When learners understand that we think with concepts, and that we connect concepts with linking words, to make statements (propositions) about how they are related, it is easy to understand "that reading is learning how to recognize printed labels for concepts and linking words" (Novak and Gowin, 1984, 26). The value of concept maps is that they help readers makes sense of what they are reading, by extracting key concepts from the printed text and organizing them in ways that show how they fit together for the reader.

Activities to develop concept map skills involve generating lists of related words to make simple statements (propositions) to connect them, e.g. *ice* is a *solid*. As students become familiar with making these relationships, they are ready to construct maps. Teachers have had success with writing concepts on index cards or construction paper so children can physically handle the concepts to construct a map. Posting sample maps on a bulletin board gives learners a chance to compare and contrast various maps. Having students work independently or in pairs to construct a map about a short story, or a paragraph from a science or social studies text is usually an effective introduction to the skill of concept mapping. By posting finished examples, it is possible to show the importance of a hierarchy on a map, and the effectiveness of appropriate linking words.

In conversations when I was writing my dissertation in the mid-Eighties, Gowin compared concept maps to "rubber sheets." They can be stretched at any point and expanded to include more concepts. This encourages students to consider thinking as a flexible and on-going process, consistent with ideas such as *advanced organizers, cognitive subsumption, progressive differentia-tion,* and *integrative reconciliation* by Ausubel, Novak, and Hanesian (1978), *adaptation* by Piaget, and *scaffolding* by Vygotsky (Morrison 2000). Concept maps contribute to *active learning, cooperative learning, authentic learning* and *authentic assessment* (Morrison 2000).

Novak and Gowin developed a scoring rubric for concept maps (1984, 36-37). The relationship between two concepts in bubbles makes a statement using connecting words, this statement is a proposition that can be affirmed or denied; therefore, the map maker must be able to substantiate the claim from the text. The hierarchy is also important. Subordinate concepts clarify those in the level above and can be given points according to Novak and Gowin. Significant cross-links, showing meaningful connections among concepts are scored for additional credit. Examples can be added to concept maps, and, finally, the teacher can construct a map that can be used as a standard. Student maps can be scored in comparison to the standard, allowing for con-struction of maps more sophisticated than the example, given higher grades than one hundred percent. Appealing to the rubric gives a means to evaluate maps. The map following the rubric gives a visual guide to scoring the maps (Figure 3.3).

1. *Propositions.* Is the meaning relationship between two concepts indicated by the connecting line and linking word (s)? Is the relationship valid? For each meaningful, valid proposition shown, score 1 point. (See scoring model below.)
2. *Hierarchy.* Does the map show hierarchy? Is each subordinate concept more specific and less general than the concept drawn above it (in the context of the material being mapped)? Score 5 points for each valid level of the hierarchy.
3. *Cross links.* Does the map show meaningful connections between one segment of the concept hierarchy and another segment? Is the relationship shown significant and valid? Score 10 points for each cross link that is both valid and significant and 2 points for each cross link that is valid but does not illustrate a synthesis between sets of related concepts or proposi-tions. Cross links can indicate creative ability and special care should be given to identifying and rewarding its expression. Unique or creative cross links might receive special recognition, or extra points.
4. *Examples.* Specific events or objects that are valid instances of those des-ignated by the concept label can be scored 1 point each. (These are not circled because they are not concepts.)
5. In addition, a criterion concept map may be constructed, and scored, for the material to be mapped, and the student scores divided by the criterion

Scoring Model

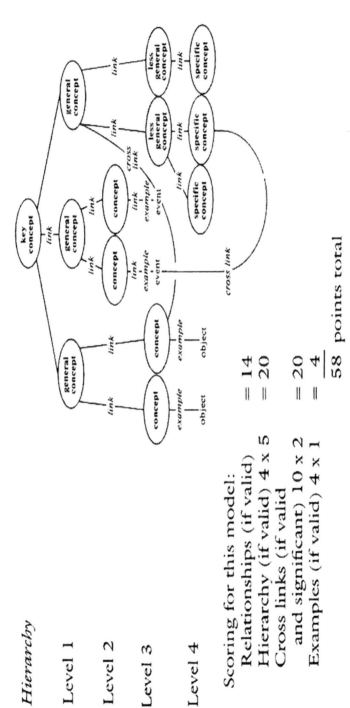

Figure 3.3. Scoring model for concept maps.

map score to give a percentage for comparison. (Some students may do better than the criterion and receive more than 100% on this basis). (Novak and Gowin 1984, 36)

After working with concept maps, a teacher gets a feel for the accuracy and complexity of maps for particular subjects, like math or science or language arts. For example, when I have students analyze a piece of literature using a concept map, it is fairly easy to assess the strengths and weaknesses of the map based on key concepts related to plot, characters and action of the novel. The mechanics of the concept map, e.g. the linking words, the hierarchy, the accuracy of the relationships and the overall flow of the map are quite clear when one sees a sample of strong and weak ones. Letter grades are then easy to determine.

AESOP AND *OH, THE PLACES YOU'LL GO*

The lesson to teach concept mapping summarized previously, I use with elementary students in grades three through six in a summer language arts program at Stetson University that I call AESOP: Authentic Educating Summer Opportunity Program. For several summers, we associated our program with CHESS (Challenges for Elementary School Students) in conjunction with the Belin Blank International Center for Gifted and Talented Education at the University of Iowa, directed by Nicholas Colangelo. Nick's *Handbook of Gifted Education* (2003) is an excellent collection of recent research about educating gifted students.

When Nick and I were friends in college, then later in graduate school after we taught for several years, we talked often about what kind of educating we would like to see in schools. The CHESS model incorporates many ideas that we talked about over the past forty years, and the AESOP model adds the dimension of authentic educating.

AESOP class size is small. The maximum is twenty students. The aim is to develop interesting curriculum and get students involved in active learning with appropriate materials. My experiences with AESOP are some of my most enjoyable teaching, and students agree that the program has offered some of their most valuable learning experiences.

In contrast, I hear my undergraduate students return from field experience in local schools saying that kids look bored, and that teachers seem overwhelmed by all the restrictions that force them to focus on standardized test results. I hear classroom teachers in my graduate courses complain that what brought them into teaching—interest in working with children and teaching meaningful things—is sacrificed by legislation that mandates curriculum. Clearly, a large amount of what goes on in schools these days is drudgery for both students and teachers, a significant concern for those of us who believe that education can be meaningful and enjoyable.

I wonder how legislators would feel if they were required to teach for a month in our public schools. If the President or governor or legislators were required to teach in a public school for a month, how would they do? After the first week, would they be pleading for a veteran teacher with whom to co-teach, pleading for less restrictions and prescriptions, smaller classes? I invite state or federal legislators to observe in an AESOP classroom, or teach in one for a few weeks. Then I would like to see how they feel about their form of educating and authentic educating.

When I hear my best undergraduate students say that after observing in schools, they wonder how long they can endure as teachers, I worry. Or, when my graduate students, who have been teaching several years, say they are leaving to pursue other careers, I worry about the future of American education.

It is distressing that a recent study found half the college graduates with teaching degrees choose not to go into teaching, and more than twenty percent who take their degree into the schools leave the field within three years. Somehow, those mandating what happens in schools have got to get a much better understanding of the day to day impact their legislation has on lives of teachers and students.

Thousands of teachers will retire in the next few years. The prognosis is that there will be a huge shortage of teachers nationally. There already is a shortage nationally and in Florida. It is not hard to see what drives people out of teaching, nor is it hard to see what could lure them back. If legislators were to try their mandates in classrooms as teachers, it would not take long for them to want to open dialogues about compromise, common ground, and change.

Teaching in AESOP is interesting and enjoyable. I teach it in a thirty hour format: two weeks for three hours a day, or one week for six hours a day. I share some of what I teach to introductory education majors with a group of third through sixth graders. We start with philosophy, do poetry, and literature, and finish with one-act plays that they perform in our classroom for parents and guests or that they videotape, edit and burn to CD or DVD and show on the big screen in the classroom and distribute copies.

If you are wondering what the general profile of the twenty students in the group was on the philosophy inventory, most had progressivism or existentialism as their top choice. Their profiles were similar to the profile of most students at the university, and the random sample we used to standardize the instrument (Griffis 1998), and the majority of teachers in the field (King 2000; Dailey 2002). So, it is not hard to understand why I believe that authentic educating should have appeal to students and teachers. I continue to be amazed that legislators insist upon essentialist curriculum and do not understand how that uncompromising stand could be driving students to drop out of school and teachers to leave the field.

To emphasize my point further, after conversations with Roger Johnson (Eggen and Kauchak 2004), who developed cooperative learning, I appreciate the social aspects of cooperative learning and the active learning it involves when done well, but similar progressive ideas have been around since Dewey. And after conversations with Howard Gardner, who developed the theory of multiple intelligences (Eggen and Kauchak 2004), I believe that involving students in active learning that engages them intellectually and emotionally—whether one calls the intelligences Gardner defines beyond mathematical-logical and linguistic intelligence intelligences or talents—to expand education beyond traditional curriculum is crucial.

Since Gardner added a ninth intelligence to his theory—existential intelligence—there is support in his theory for the value of authentic educating as a philosophic perspective. But philosophers have argued since Plato about the importance of educating people based upon their range of talent. Therefore, involving students in authentic educating can be more valuable than cooperative learning and multiple intelligences theory, with which I am sympathetic, because authentic educating engages students in progressive and existential ideas that aim them toward cognitive, emotional and philosophic growth.

To introduce AESOP students to concept mapping, I used *Oh, The Places You'll Go!* by Dr. Seuss (1990). I distribute a copy of the book to each pair of students, and ask them to read out loud with the class. The rules guiding this exercise are that everyone has to participate, and that I would not call on anyone, but whenever there is silence, a student starts reading. If there are suddenly multiple readers, each is to be considerate and let one person read, but be ready and eager to jump into the next silence, until everyone reads. After everyone reads, there are additional opportunities. Finally, one could not read more than a page at a time. There are multiple ways to do an exercise like this, but I want students to feel they can participate without me having to monitor them. Students should look out for themselves and each other.

When everyone is finished, I ask students to find a passage that they like, and rehearse it for a few minutes. Then I ask for volunteers to *recite*. This allows for an entertaining change of pace, as they stand and recite Dr. Seuss' colorful language. It also gives me a chance to see who might need some encouragement later on when we start rehearsing to perform the one-act plays based on the novels. I notice, however, that many more AESOP students volunteer than when I make the same offer to my undergraduate students. Most of these elementary school kids loved to perform.

Afterwards, I ask them to construct a concept map about the story. Students had about forty-five minutes to read, recite, and concept map the story. For their first attempts at mapping literature, I supply them with markers and paper. Since this was the students' first experience with concept mapping, there was no need to assign a letter grade. Instead, as students completed their maps, I had them use masking tape to post their signed work on the back wall, so, that when everyone was finished, we could have a gallery show and assess the strengths and weaknesses of the posted maps.

The map is by two fourth graders (Figure 3.4). They have a good feel for the action. The students used drawing tools in PowerPoint to construct this map. Teaching them how to use this software took about a half-hour. Constructing their hand drawn map took about a half-hour and translating it into this graphic took about an hour. It is quite sophisticated, but does not resolve the theme of the novel.

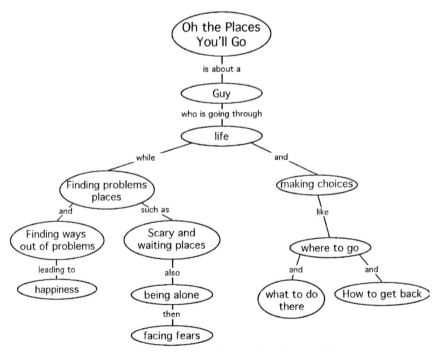

Figure 3.4. Fourth graders' concept map for *Oh the Places You'll Go*.

Early concept maps show that students understand the skills required in concept mapping, and can use maps to summarize what they have read. They are able to make a distinction between the good and bad places that Dr. Seuss identified. Further, they get a sense of the action of the short novel, and the way the key character confronts and resolves his situation.

This sample shows that students can use concept maps to extract meaning from the text. Sharing reading out loud, while showing each other the colorful illustrations, makes for an amusing, non-threatening reading experience, and a chance for the teacher to circulate around the room unobtrusively, to listen for skill and comfort level. Having the students construct the map as a pair requires that they discuss key elements of the story in order to identify key concepts from which to make the map. This helps them focus and remember what they read. Since I like color maps, as I mentioned before, I usually have colored markers and extra sheets of standard size photocopy paper available. This way, students are able to draw several drafts, until they get the map the way they like it aesthetically. Negotiating the form and content of the maps furthers discussion. If a pair of students cannot reach agreement on a map, I allow individuals to construct a map. However, students rarely choose this option.

When all students were finished constructing their maps, we had a gallery show of their work on the back wall. They each got to see all maps, and then to vote on which they believed were the strongest. This allows for discussion of strengths of particular maps, and suggestions for improvement. I focus discussion on establishing a hierarchy, making distinctions based on the text, and using only key concepts that appear in print in the text, and use of connecting words so that anyone can read the map and understand what the map maker is trying to convey. Surely, the kids whose maps are chosen as strongest enjoy the attention. But those whose maps need work begin to see how they can improve. I've yet to have students say that not having their work voted strongest was traumatic, but many have said how they can see how to make better maps.

MAPPING LITERATURE

To emphasize literature, I showed students samples of Henry David Thoreau's journal (Shepard 1961). We discuss the following excerpt in detail. I have them read it first, then to discuss it with a partner to see what they thought Thoreau meant. Many focus on the idea that Thoreau believed that one needed to be prepared for learning, to have some prior experience in order to learn new things. This perspective fits quite well into the work of

Ausubel, Piaget and Vygotsky. Ausubel claimed the "the most important single factor influencing learning is what the learner already knows" (Novak and Gowin 1984, 122). Thoreau seemed to agree.

> Jan. 5, 1860
>
> A man receives only what he is ready to receive, whether physically or intellectually or morally, as animals conceive at certain seasons their kind only. We hear and apprehend only what we already half know. If there is something which does not concern me, which is out of my line, which by experience or by genius my attention is not drawn to, however novel and remarkable it may be, if it is spoken, we hear it not, if it is written, we read it not, or if we read it, it does not detain us. Every man thus *tracks himself* through life, in all his hearing and reading and observation and traveling. His observations make a chain. (Shepard 1961, 212)

One summer, after discussing Thoreau's journal, I showed students newspaper articles from the *Daytona News Journal* and the *Orlando Sentinel* about celebrations of Ernest Hemingway's hundredth birthday (1899-1999). Afterwards, I played a recording of Hemingway reading his Nobel Prize acceptance speech (Caedmon 1965).

> Having no facility for speech-making and no command of oratory nor any domination of rhetoric, I wish to thank the administrators of the generosity of Alfred Nobel for this prize.
>
> No writer who knows the great writers who did not receive the prize can accept it other than with humility. There is no need to list these writers. Everyone here may make his own list according to his knowledge and his conscience.
>
> It would be impossible for me to ask the Ambassador of my country to read a speech in which a writer said all of the things which are in his heart. Things may not be immediately discernible in what a man writes, and in this sometimes he is fortunate; but eventually they are quite clear and by these and the degree of alchemy that he possesses he will endure or be forgotten.
>
> Writing, at its best, is a lonely life. Organizations for writers palliate the writer's loneliness but I doubt if they improve his writing. He grows in public stature as he sheds his loneliness and often his work deteriorates. For he does his work alone and if he is a good enough writer he must face eternity, or the lack of it, each day.
>
> For a true writer each book should be a new beginning where he tries again for something that is beyond attainment. He should always try for something that has never been done or that others have tried and failed. Then sometimes, with great luck, he will succeed.
>
> How simple the writing of literature would be if it were only necessary to write in another way what has been well written. It is because we have had such

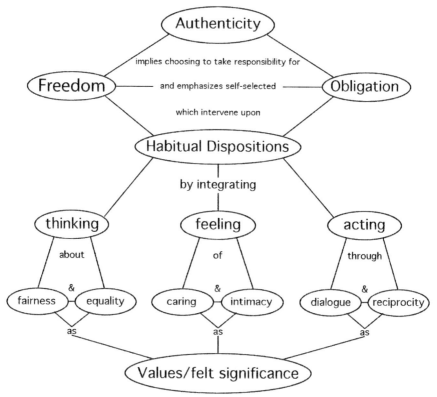

Figure 3.5. Concept map for authenticity.

great writers in the past that a writer is driven far out past where he can go, out
to where no one can help him.

I have spoken too long for a writer. A writer should write what he has to say
and not speak it. Again I thank you. (Baker 1968, 669)

Discussion centers on challenges that writers face writing literature. Students mention that Hemingway seemed humble about the difficulty of writing well, even though he experienced great success. Several students took Hemingway's challenge and offered to write an original play during one summer session. After we discuss the speech, I show students the concept map about authenticity, from Chapter 1 (Figure 3.5) to prepare them to assess the characters in the novels we were to read.

I show college students' responses to a quiz question that asked them to define authenticity. These undergraduate students had been in a course I taught about authentic educating. Their answers to the quiz are as follows:

Quiz Question: Define Authenticity

Authenticity is being true to yourself, and to do that, you must be in touch with your innermost feelings. Being authentic means choosing obligations. To be an authentic person, you must care about other people and respect their authenticity, which means letting them have their way sometimes, so they don't have to sacrifice their authenticity for you.
  Emilie

Authenticity, to the best of my knowledge, includes acting in a way that is true to one's self, maintaining reciprocal, caring relationships with others, and taking responsibility for one's actions.
  Carra

After the discussion to prepare AESOP students to read the novels, I read excerpts from the novel covers and give students time to page through the novels so they could select which of them they wanted to read. That morning, they start reading, knowing they were trying to look at authenticity of the characters, and toward concept mapping the story to prepare a script for a one-act play.

The map (Figure 3.6) summarizes the action of *The Cay* (Taylor 1969), a novel about a young white boy stranded on an island with an African-American man after a shipwreck. The two fifth graders focus on the main character Phillip's prejudice prior to the accident, based on attitudes he had developed

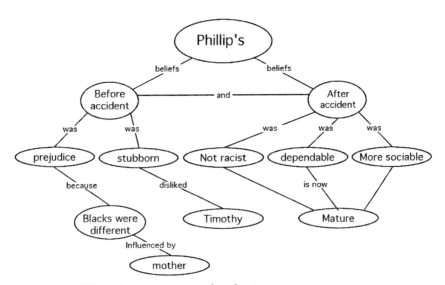

Figure 3.6.   Fifth graders' concept map for *The Cay*.

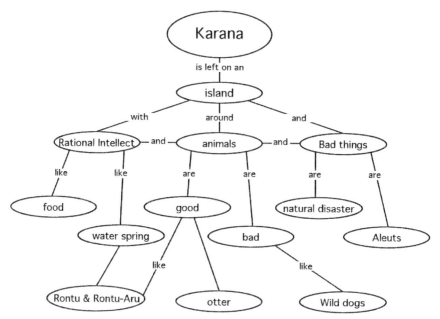

Figure 3.7. Sixth graders' concept map for *Island of the Blue Dolphins*.

from his mother's prejudice. After the accident, and his experience with the black man Timothy, Phillip's attitude changes.

The map (Figure 3.7) constructed by two sixth grade students summarizes *Island of the Blue Dolphin* (O'Dell 1960), which chronicles the maturing of a young Native American girl on an island off the California coast. The quality of the map is quite impressive.

The plot of *The Old Man and the Sea* (Hemingway 1952) shows an old Cuban fisherman's struggle with a giant marlin. Three AESOP students, who performed the play, summarize the novel in their concept map (Figure 3.8). They identify Santiago as the main character and sketch his relationship with Manolin and the marlin. During their preparation of the play, I discussed with them that the Hemingway hero shows "grace under pressure" (Kaplin 1992, 701). The students understood this by identifying the respect that Santiago has for the struggle he endures.

As students read the novels during the summer session, I help them concept map the plot, and my graduate students and I work with them to transfer their maps to PowerPoint for presentation to parents and guests on the day of the play. We discussed the concept of authenticity and moved to discussion of the learning Vee, which is described in the next chapter. As the students maintained personal journals about an issue of authenticity in their lives, read their

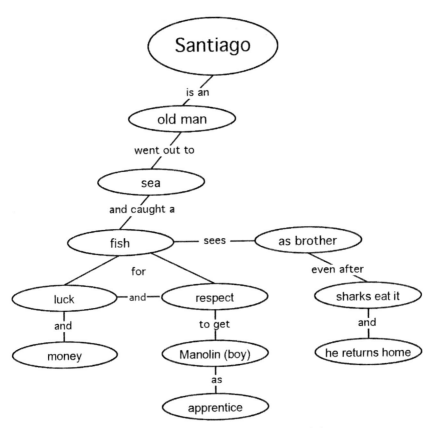

Figure 3.8.   **Fifth graders' concept map for *The Old Man and the Sea*.**

novels and prepared a script for their one-act plays, we met in small groups. They posted their concept maps and Vee diagrams and the evolving scripts for their one act plays on the wall in the classroom. We worked between the classroom and the computer lab next door, so that all their work would be computer processed.

Towards the last few of the ten day summer program, there is a lot to accomplish. Rehearsals for the plays start in the room. I set off a section of the room, by attaching an old sheet to the ceiling as a drape to define a stage. Because of the novel settings, students drew a tropical scene as the backdrop for the stage, using a sheet of butcher-block paper. We decorated the stage with some large plants from my office, and we used a wooden table from the main lobby for the boats in the novels. Students work at home to prepare their costumes. The final day of the summer session we stage the one-act plays.

The challenge I posed to students for the play was that they had to condense the novel plot into a ten-minute play. Each member of the group had to participate, either as actor or narrator, and they had to stay true to the text, using the author's words whenever they could. This required that they all read their novel. But further, after concept mapping it, and trying to answer the question "Does the character move toward authenticity?" using the learning Vee, they had to extract the essence of the book and perform it for parents and guests on the last day. One summer, we had a room full, including Vince Carter's mom.

Vince Carter was the 1999 Rookie of the Year in the National Basketball Association (NBA). He graduated from Mainland High School in Daytona Beach, before playing college basketball at the University of North Carolina. His mother, Michelle Carter-Robinson was a Volusia County teacher while he was growing up. She is the Director of his philanthropic organization called *The Embassy of Hope*. As Embassy Director, graciously she donated money to help support students in financial need to attend the summer program. The first day of the program, we showed parents and students a videotape of Vince Carter, who was taking summer courses at the University of North Carolina—to complete the degree he promised his mother he would finish. The videotape, titled *Soaring to New Heights* is a six minute highlight film of Vince's career, from when he was an elementary school student, to his incredible spinning jams in the NBA as Rookie of the Year. The video ends with Vince stressing the importance of school, and mentors, like his coach Charles Brinkerhoff—who was a graduate student of mine at Stetson and introduced me to Vince—whom Vince thanked for the powerful influence *Coach Brink* had on his life.

I was particularly interested that Mrs. Carter-Robinson see the student plays, especially production of Theodore Taylor's *The* Cay (1969). I met Theodore Taylor in 1996, at a Children's Literature Conference sponsored by Stetson's Department of Teacher Education. Without a clue to what he looked like, I volunteered to pick him up at DeLand's Holiday Inn, to bring him to the conference as the keynote speaker. Among the various people in the lobby that morning, only he looked like a writer. He wore a faded blue shirt, had silver hair and mustache, and a canvas bag, full of books and notes. He was a wiry fellow in his mid-seventies, with a strong handshake, an amiable manner, and intense blue eyes. As we chatted during the short drive to the university, I was impressed by his eagerness toward the conference, and passion about his writing.

When I asked him about influences on his writing, he mentioned Mark Twain adamantly. He seemed to agree with Hemingway, that American literature really started with Mark Twain. He also talked about the writer's responsibility to have a positive influence through writing. When one considers the theme in *The Cay*, it is clear that Taylor was dealing with issues similar to Mark Twain in *Huckleberry Finn*. Phillip and Timothy are reminiscent of Huck and Jim . . . and there are shipwrecks and rafts—and continued prejudice in the world for writers to confront.

In the short script that the students prepared, they saw what Taylor was getting at. In the play, performed by four girls, Lynesha, who played Timothy, was the only African-American. And after all the reading, and concept mapping, and learning Vees about authenticity, what counted was the way those third through sixth grade students rehearsed and acted the script. My feeling is they learned what Taylor was getting at when Lynesah protected the girl playing Phillip during the noise and flashing lights of the hurricane acted in front of an audience of students, families and friends. Extracting the essence of Taylor's novel into a short play, rehearsed hurriedly for an audience, they got a sense of what he intended by working with each other during the last few days, relying on each other, and performing together. This is the essence of authentic educating.

Hopefully, in this chapter, you see the value of concept mapping, and how it can be used in the classroom. But as I write about authentic educating, I hope you are beginning to see that it involves much more than concept mapping. The various exercises I described in this chapter are key to authentic educating, but the genuine aim is to have students integrate their thinking, feeling and acting. They need to understand how to solve problems, and read and extract information from texts, but they also need to work with the teacher and each other to move toward authenticity, by taking personal responsibility for themselves, and having some fun in the process. I believe authentic educating relies on a sound philosophical foundation, but authentic educating also means that learning can and should be fun.

Learning about philosophy, literature, the heuristic tools of concept mapping and the Vee, and preparing PowerPoint presentations, scripts, scenery, costumes and props, and performing to an audience is a lot to accomplish in thirty hours, but they seem quite proud and happy about all they went through—maybe there is something to be said for authentic educating.

REVIEW AND REFLECT

1. Read any of the novels mentioned in this chapter and construct your own concept map of the plot.
2. Select a section from any textbook in a course you are taking or teaching. Show 7-9 key concepts in a concept map.

3. Plan a short lesson using a concept map as one of the activities.
4. Select a novel from the following list. Read it and write a reaction paper that you share with two or three others.

> Angelou, M. *I Know Why the Caged Bird Sings*
> Austen, J. *Pride and Prejudice*
> Camus, A. *The Stranger*
> Chopin, K. *The Awakening*
> Hemingway, E. *The Old Man and the Sea*
> Hurston, Z.N. *Their Eyes Were Watching God*
> McMillan, T. *Waiting to Exhale*
> Morrison, T. *Sula*
> O'Dell S. *Island of the Blue Dolphins*
> Rousseau, J.J. *Emile*
> Seuss, Dr. *Oh, The Places You'll Go*
> Tan, A. *The Joy Luck Club*
> Taylor, T. *The Cay*
> Walker, A. *The Temple of My Familiar*
> Welty, E. *The Optimist's Daughter*
> Williams, M. *The Velveteen Rabbit*

5. Select a character from the novel you read. In a well-constructed essay of about five hundred words, identify the key conflicts that the character experiences.
6. Construct a concept map that describes the major conflict the main character experiences in the novel you read.
7. Using Figure 3.5 Concept Map for Authenticity, write a paragraph about the character's struggle toward authenticity in the novel.
8. Imagine you are preparing a lesson in your field. Construct a concept map that identifies 7-9 concepts that you want to teach.
9. Plan at least two activities for the lesson you identified in #8 that will involve students in active learning and produce a personal and academic product.
10. Using your personal journal, reflect on the strengths and weaknesses of concept mapping as a tool in your teaching.

Chapter Four

The Vee as a Learning Tool

Concept mapping is one technique that Novak and Gowin (1981, 1984) developed to show relationships among key concepts under consideration. The Vee is a more sophisticated and powerful tool that can incorporate concept maps, but it was designed to show the structure of knowledge developed to answer a telling question. To extend the relationship of particular concepts to a broader view of knowledge in a discipline, Gowin developed an approach to the structure of knowledge that he summarized with five questions he called the Q-5 (Gowin 1981, 88).

1. The telling question [also called "focus question"]. What is the telling question of the work?
2. The key concepts. Conceptual structure. What are the key concepts?
3. Methods. What methods were used to answer the telling question?
4. Knowledge claims. What are the major claims in the work?
5. Value claims. What value claims are made in the work?

The telling question organizes a study and points the direction of the inquiry. The key concepts name what is to be studied. The method tells how to proceed, in other words, what to do. The knowledge claims answer the telling question, based on a summary of records. The value claims assert the worth of the knowledge. By applying these five questions to an event under consideration, it is possible to assess the structure of knowledge in a research study, a class lecture, or a curriculum.

By analyzing the structure of knowledge, one grasps how it fits together. The analysis of the structure of knowledge is facilitated by Gowin's learning Vee. The Vee is designed to show relationships among the parts under consideration, in both a conceptual and visual way. Gowin chose the Vee shape, so that the open end, the top of the Vee poses a question that aims the bottom of the Vee toward a particular event to be studied.

The Vee can be summarized as follows: the telling question directs our inquiry toward particular events that are considered. It is a question that focuses the investigation. It contains at least two key concepts within the search, and, if it is a good question, it should lead to further exploration. The exploration of events proceeds on *theoretical/conceptual* grounds and along *methodological grounds*.

On the left, the *theoretical/conceptual* side of the Vee, concepts name particular events under consideration. Concepts can be further organized after being identified and lead to principles. Principles state relationships between two or more key concepts, and can be tested in ways that confirm or deny them, similar to a hypothesis in a science experiment. For example, in the statement "heat causes ice to melt", the concept of heat is connected to ice in a causal relationship, such that the application of a heat source, like a candle or gas flame, is evaluated as a means to cause the ice to melt. The evidence could be gathered over time in a controlled experiment, and the results would support accuracy of the claim: the principle. A principle tells how concepts are connected and clarifies their meaning.

When several principles can be organized to make predictions about the world, they generate a theory that describes the events under consideration at a higher, more comprehensive, conceptual level. For example, Darwin's Theory of Evolution is comprised of principles that claim new species originate from previous species; that species adapt to the environment through random selection, and those best adapted to the environment survive. Theories help comprise a philosophy, which is the next higher level of comprehension for the concepts and events under consideration. Consequently, as one moves from the lowest level of the Vee, naming of concepts, to the highest level, organizing events into a comprehensive view, one moves from lower to higher levels of conceptual thinking.

The *methodological* side of the Vee tells what is done with the events and objects under consideration in a study. The methods used support the conceptual claims on the left side of the Vee. At the lowest level, closest to observing and naming the events, records are made to define the concepts. This gives an empirical basis to the meaning of concepts used in a study. Records are collected and organized and then transformed by summarizing them into intelligible data.

The transformations can be in the form of charts and graphs to simplify the collected information or a summary of records based on observations in the classroom or of quotes from the text of a novel to describe a character's actions. The transformed data is used to support the knowledge claims that explain the events under consideration. In a well-constructed study, the results of investigation yield information based on accurate observation of events. The transformed results are what one can claim to know from a study.

Based on knowledge claims that are derived during a study, value claims are made. A value claim tells about the worth of what is being investigated. For example, in a study that makes a knowledge claim that there is a high correlation between high levels of cholesterol in the body and heart attacks, the value claim could be that people should try to lower cholesterol in their diet. The value claim on the right side of the Vee connects to the left side of the Vee at the theoretical level to explain heart attacks, and leads toward philosophic claims about how to improve the quality of one's life.

There is active interplay between both sides of the Vee and from the lowest to the highest levels. This means that evidence from the methodological side of the Vee supports claims made on the conceptual side of the Vee and vice versa. This active interplay helps to construct a conceptual framework for a study. And this interplay generates a way in which the methods can be carried out to yield verifiable records that can be transformed to make knowledge and value claims that answer the original telling question. Below is Gowin's Vee heuristic from *Learning How to Learn* (Figure 4.1).

The next Vee (Figure 4.2) was designed to answer the telling question "Why is a curriculum integrating philosophy, literature and educating of value?" This Vee that was presented in Chapter 1 gives direction to this study about the value of authentic educating.

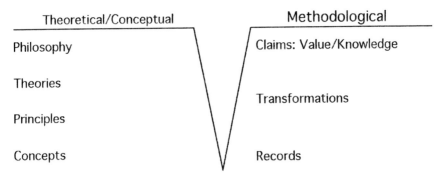

Focus Question: answers require an active interplay between the Theoretical/Conceptual and Methodological sides of the Vee.

Theoretical/Conceptual   Methodological

Philosophy   Claims: Value/Knowledge

Theories
                                Transformations
Principles

Concepts   Records

Gowin's Learning Vee heuristic illustrates the conceptual and methodological elements that interact in the process of knowledge construction (p. 3, Learning How to Learn)

Figure 4.1.   Gowin's Vee heuristic.

The focus question guides the research involved in writing this book. The event during the past twenty-five years of research was to define and assess authentic educating as a theoretical and practical guide to educating. The left side of the Vee is the conceptual side, starting at the bottom with the concepts from the concept map in Chapter 1 listed in the lower left. The principles are statements in the map and listed in the Vee. The theory summarizes the principles, and the philosophy makes a comprehensive statement about authentic educating.

On the right side of the Vee, the methods to answer the question are summarized. Records come from philosophy, literature and educational practice in the classroom. They are summarized, and these transformations of records lead to knowledge and value claims. Using the Vee heuristic allows twenty-five years of research to be summarized in a single figure.

I believe the strength of Gowin's *Educating* (1981) is his focus on defining the four commonplaces of educating: teaching, learning, curriculum, and governance, and the heuristic tools he introduces. Novak and Gowin's *Learning How to Learn* (1984) describes how to use these tools in the classroom and to guide research. As I develop my view of authentic educating, the concept map and Vee help define the direction of my research.

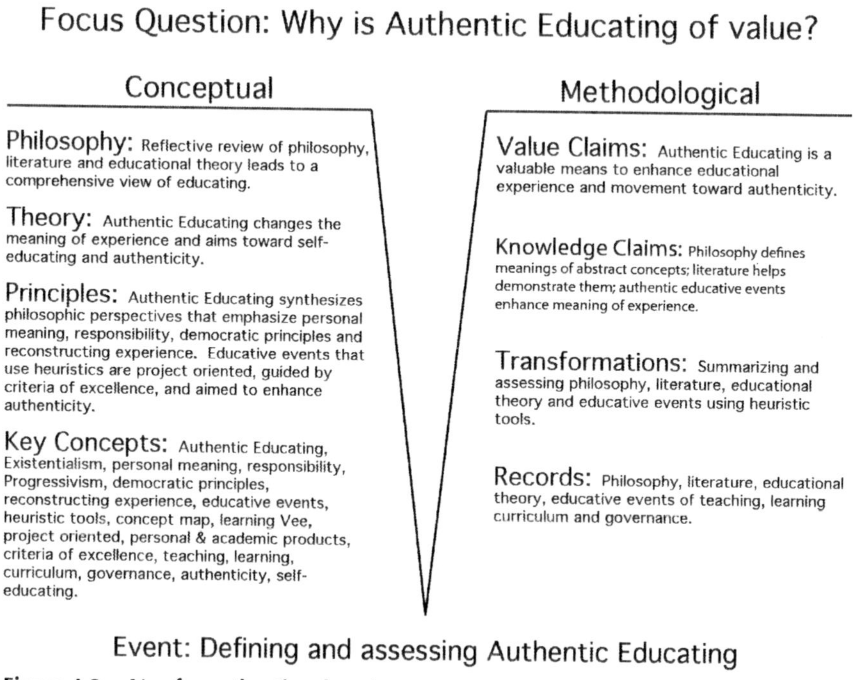

Focus Question: Why is Authentic Educating of value?

Conceptual

Philosophy: Reflective review of philosophy, literature and educational theory leads to a comprehensive view of educating.

Theory: Authentic Educating changes the meaning of experience and aims toward self-educating and authenticity.

Principles: Authentic Educating synthesizes philosophic perspectives that emphasize personal meaning, responsibility, democratic principles and reconstructing experience. Educative events that use heuristics are project oriented, guided by criteria of excellence, and aimed to enhance authenticity.

Key Concepts: Authentic Educating, Existentialism, personal meaning, Progressivism, democratic principles, reconstructing experience, educative events, heuristic tools, concept map, learning Vee, project oriented, personal & academic products, criteria of excellence, teaching, learning, curriculum, governance, authenticity, self-educating.

Methodological

Value Claims: Authentic Educating is a valuable means to enhance educational experience and movement toward authenticity.

Knowledge Claims: Philosophy defines meanings of abstract concepts; literature helps demonstrate them; authentic educative events enhance meaning of experience.

Transformations: Summarizing and assessing philosophy, literature, educational theory and educative events using heuristic tools.

Records: Philosophy, literature, educational theory, educative events of teaching, learning curriculum and governance.

Event: Defining and assessing Authentic Educating

Figure 4.2. Vee for authentic educating.

USING CONCEPT MAPS AND VEES

The concept map and Vee complement each other. After reading material in any subject, students extract key concepts in order to summarize what they read. A well constructed concept map shows relationships among concepts in the reading. Formulating a telling question using key concepts helps students construct a comprehensive answer to questions about the reading.

The following concept map and Vee are from a presentation about Plato's myth of the metals that accounts for the differences among people in *The Republic*. The excerpt from *The Republic* that it is based on appears in Steven Cahn's *Classic and Contemporary Readings in the Philosophy of Education* (1997). The concept map and Vee (Figures 4.3 and 4.4) were made in PowerPoint, and the student presented them in an undergraduate philosophy of education course. His presentation was videotaped then inserted into the PowerPoint and stored on compact disk (CD) and digital videodisk (DVD) to be used as an example for others.

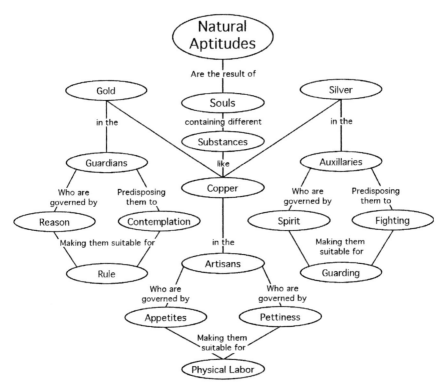

Figure 4.3. Concept map for Plato's myth of the metals.

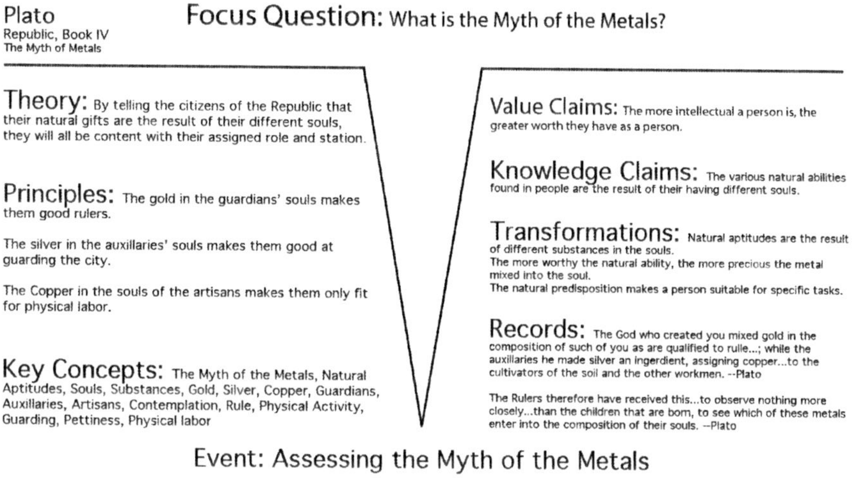

Plato   Focus Question: What is the Myth of the Metals?
Republic, Book IV
The Myth of Metals

Theory: By telling the citizens of the Republic that their natural gifts are the result of their different souls, they will all be content with their assigned role and station.

Value Claims: The more intellectual a person is, the greater worth they have as a person.

Knowledge Claims: The various natural abilities found in people are the result of their having different souls.

Principles: The gold in the guardians' souls makes them good rulers.

The silver in the auxillaries' souls makes them good at guarding the city.

The Copper in the souls of the artisans makes them only fit for physical labor.

Transformations: Natural aptitudes are the result of different substances in the souls.
The more worthy the natural ability, the more precious the metal mixed into the soul.
The natural predisposition makes a person suitable for specific tasks.

Records: The God who created you mixed gold in the composition of such of you as are qualified to rule...; while the auxillaries he made silver an ingerdient, assigning copper...to the cultivators of the soil and the other workmen. --Plato

The Rulers therefore have received this...to observe nothing more closely...than the children that are born, to see which of these metals enter into the composition of their souls. --Plato

Key Concepts: The Myth of the Metals, Natural Aptitudes, Souls, Substances, Gold, Silver, Copper, Guardians, Auxillaries, Artisans, Contemplation, Rule, Physical Activity, Guarding, Pettiness, Physical labor

Event: Assessing the Myth of the Metals

Figure 4.4.   Vee for Plato's myth of the metals.

As he indicates, Plato makes an argument for the republic to be ruled by the guardians, which Plato identified as the philosopher kings. For Plato, his argument is based on natural characteristics of souls that are contained for a time in mortal bodies. It is a metaphysical argument about the nature of humans, and drove Plato's theory of educating in the republic as he envisioned it. It seems to me that his form of elitism is contrary to the aims of authentic educating in a democracy, and clearly, Plato was antagonistic to democratic education.

In the Vee (Figure 4.4), the telling question at the top points the bottom of the Vee to the events under consideration. The increasing width of the Vee at the top signifies a more comprehensive viewpoint is achieved at higher conceptual levels of theory and method. By using the concepts from the map, Nathan is able to construct the principles about the various metals and thus show the myth that drives Plato's argument. In this way, the theory implies that there would be harmony in the republic if people were to accept their place based on the characteristics of their souls.

On the right side of the Vee, excerpts from the text show what Plato says in *The Republic* to support his argument. Selecting and summarizing Plato's words gives support to answer the question about the myth and the knowledge and value claims that answer the question. The concept map and Vee heuristics help guide students to construct sophisticated summaries and analyses of what they read.

The following example is about Margery Williams' *The Velveteen Rabbit* (1981). The concept map summarizes the children's novel about the

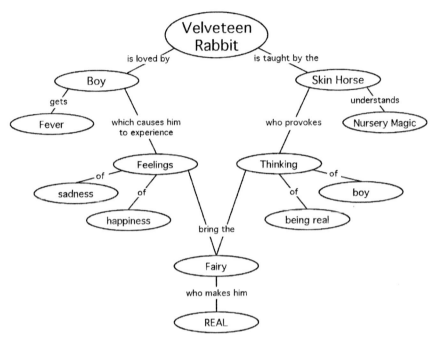

Figure 4.5. Concept map for *The Velveteen Rabbit*.

relationship between a boy and his toy Velveteen rabbit that is transformed by nursery magic into a real bunny (Figure 4.5).

To answer the question, "How does the Velveteen Rabbit become authentic?" four students—who created a script from the novel to perform a one-act play for fellow undergraduate students enrolled in an introductory education course—constructed the following Vee diagram (Figure 4.6). The left side contains concepts from the map to form principles about the story that are supported on the right side as records based on excerpts from the text. Construction of the Vee allows the students to make knowledge and value claims about the story and to develop a theory about movement toward authenticity.

The following concept map and Vee (Figures 4.7 and 4.8) summarize Theodore Taylor's *The Cay* (1969). It is a popular novel for middle school that intrigues undergraduate students as they assess the main character Phillip's movement toward authenticity and perform the novel as a one-act play. It is during preparation of the play and the concept maps and Vees that students get to work with each other. The learning tools help them assess the plot of the novel and the characters, and the Vee helps them to assess the question about the character's movement toward authenticity. In addition, preparation for the play requires that students consider the five principles of

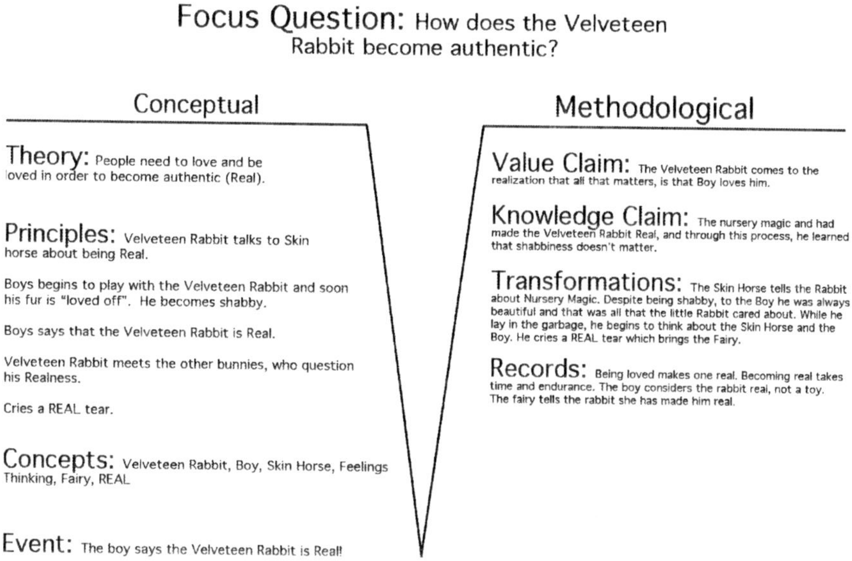

Focus Question: How does the Velveteen
Rabbit become authentic?

Conceptual	Methodological

Theory: People need to love and be loved in order to become authentic (Real).

Principles: Velveteen Rabbit talks to Skin horse about being Real.

Boys begins to play with the Velveteen Rabbit and soon his fur is "loved off". He becomes shabby.

Boys says that the Velveteen Rabbit is Real.

Velveteen Rabbit meets the other bunnies, who question his Realness.

Cries a REAL tear.

Concepts: Velveteen Rabbit, Boy, Skin Horse, Feelings Thinking, Fairy, REAL

Event: The boy says the Velveteen Rabbit is Real!

Value Claim: The Velveteen Rabbit comes to the realization that all that matters, is that Boy loves him.

Knowledge Claim: The nursery magic and had made the Velveteen Rabbit Real, and through this process, he learned that shabbiness doesn't matter.

Transformations: The Skin Horse tells the Rabbit about Nursery Magic. Despite being shabby, to the Boy he was always beautiful and that was all that the little Rabbit cared about. While he lay in the garbage, he begins to think about the Skin Horse and the Boy. He cries a REAL tear which brings the Fairy.

Records: Being loved makes one real. Becoming real takes time and endurance. The boy considers the rabbit real, not a toy. The fairy tells the rabbit she has made him real.

Figure 4.6.   Vee for *The Velveteen Rabbit.*

authenticity as they work together. It is the group work that allows students to better understand the concepts of authentic educating and authenticity that they are required to write about as they evaluate their experience with the one-act play.

This map shows the racist attitudes that the boy Phillip had toward the older man, Timothy. This novel is reminiscent of Mark Twain's *Huckleberry Finn* (1996), and during a conversation I had with Theodore Taylor, when he visited our campus for a literature conference, he mentioned that Twain's writing influenced him.

The Vee is a well-constructed answer to the question "Does Phillip move toward authenticity?" On the left side of the Vee, the theoretical side, the key concepts used to answer the question are shown in the concept map, and help to form principles—statements about the relationships among two or more concepts—that support a theoretical summary of what authentic relationships entail. On the right side, the methodological side that requires evidence to support the left side, the students identify records as quotes from the text to support their principles. Moving up the Vee, they summarize the quotes by telling how Phillip changes during the novel and what they can claim to know about his transformations and the values that he shows toward the end of the novel. In this way, they construct their argument for Phillip's movement toward authenticity during the novel. The Vee is a tool for students to justify their answers to particular questions from a theoretical and practical perspective and entails high-level thinking.

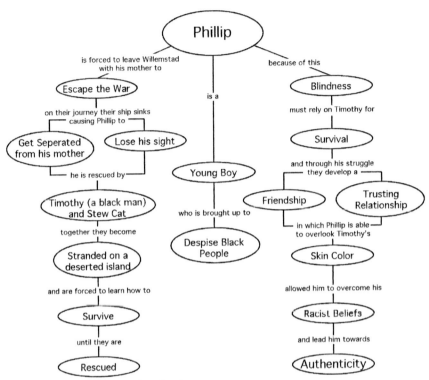

Figure 4.7.   Concept map for *The Cay*.

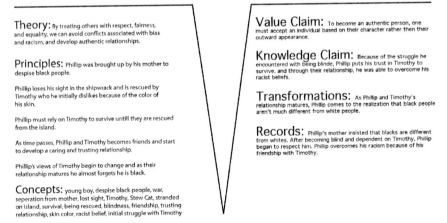

Focus Question: Does Phillip move toward Authenticity?

Theory: By treating others with respect, fairness, and equality, we can avoid conflicts associated with bias and racism, and develop authentic relationships.

Principles: Phillip was brought up by his mother to despise black people.

Phillip loses his sight in the shipwrack and is rescued by Timothy who he initially dislikes because of the color of his skin.

Phillip must rely on Timothy to survive untill they are rescued from the island.

As time passes, Phillip and Timothy becomes friends and start to develop a caring and trusting relationship.

Phillip's views of Timothy begin to change and as their relationship matures he almost forgets he is black.

Concepts: young boy, despise black people, war, seperation from mother, lost sight, Timothy, Stew Cat, stranded on island, survival, being rescued, blindness, friendship, trusting relationship, skin color, racist belief, initial struggle with Timothy

Value Claim: To become an authentic person, one must accept an individual based on their character rather then their outward appearance.

Knowledge Claim: Because of the struggle he encountered with being blinde, Phillip puts his trust in Timothy to survive, and through their relationship, he was able to overcome his racist beliefs.

Transformations: As Phillip and Timothy's relationship matures, Phillip comes to the realization that black people aren't much different from white people.

Records: Phillip's mother insisted that blacks were different from whites. After becoming blind and dependent on Timothy, Phillip began to respect him. Phillip overcomes his racism because of his friendship with Timothy.

Event: Assessing how Phillip moves toward authenticity.

Figure 4.8.   Vee for *The Cay*.

Figure 4.9. Concept map for *The Old Man and the Sea*.

The next concept map and Vee (Figures 4.9 and 4.10) summarize the Pulitzer Prize winning novel *The Old Man and the Sea* (1952) that helped Ernest Hemingway win the Nobel Prize in Literature in 1954. The map is a helpful tool to summarize the action of any novel in one page. The Vee can be used to guide any question a student has or that a teacher wants students to investigate. A character's movement toward authenticity is only one of many questions that can be answered, and authentic educating aims to help students learn ways to explore their teacher's and their own questions.

Figure 4.10 answers the question about Santiago's movement toward authenticity.

In addition to the concept map and Vee is a reaction paper that a freshman wrote to summarize her feelings about the novel. Reaction papers can be shared with other students and the instructor, and allow students to summarize key thoughts and feelings about a novel.

The Old Man and the Sea

Throughout Ernest Hemingway's novel, Santiago, an old Cuban fisherman, struggled to defeat a huge marlin. The old man went days without a single catch, but on his final journey through the sea, he found himself faced with

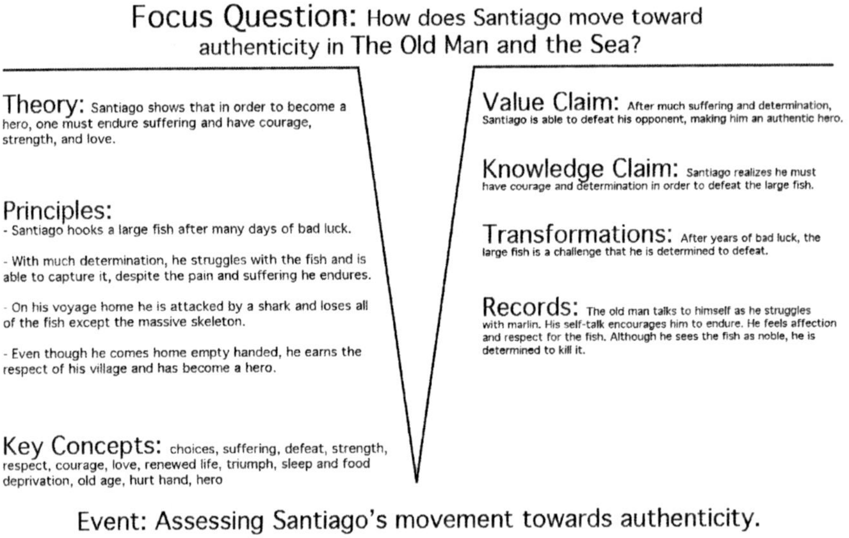

Focus Question: How does Santiago move toward authenticity in The Old Man and the Sea?

Theory: Santiago shows that in order to become a hero, one must endure suffering and have courage, strength, and love.

Value Claim: After much suffering and determination, Santiago is able to defeat his opponent, making him an authentic hero.

Knowledge Claim: Santiago realizes he must have courage and determination in order to defeat the large fish.

Principles:
- Santiago hooks a large fish after many days of bad luck.

- With much determination, he struggles with the fish and is able to capture it, despite the pain and suffering he endures.

- On his voyage home he is attacked by a shark and loses all of the fish except the massive skeleton.

- Even though he comes home empty handed, he earns the respect of his village and has become a hero.

Transformations: After years of bad luck, the large fish is a challenge that he is determined to defeat.

Records: The old man talks to himself as he struggles with marlin. His self-talk encourages him to endure. He feels affection and respect for the fish. Although he sees the fish as noble, he is determined to kill it.

Key Concepts: choices, suffering, defeat, strength, respect, courage, love, renewed life, triumph, sleep and food deprivation, old age, hurt hand, hero

Event: Assessing Santiago's movement towards authenticity.

Figure 4.10. Vee for *The Old Man and the Sea*.

the largest challenge of all: reeling in a massive fish alone. The struggle with his opponent went for three days as Santiago battled and suffered through old age, lack of sleep and food, and a hurt hand. He finally defeated the fish proving his strength, courage, respect, and love. As he traveled back home, a couple of sharks attacked him and his beloved fish. The sharks ate most of his fish, leaving only the bones as proof of Santiago's catch. When he got back to the village, many thought that he had caught a shark, but they realized that it was, in fact, a very large fish. Everyone was impressed by Santiago's accomplishments and respected him for his courage. He had become a true hero of his village.

Santiago moved towards authenticity, as he became the village hero. He demonstrates that in order to become a hero, one must endure much suffering with determination. Hemingway says that Santiago was determined to win the struggle, which suggests that no matter what Santiago endured, he would not give up until he defeated his opponent. I believe this novel is motivational because we should all try to stay determined until success.

The following figures (Figure 4.11 and 4.12) summarize a study conducted by a high school chemistry teacher for his Master's thesis. The abstract summarizes the project, and the related concept map and Vee gives an overview of the study. Hugh "Chris" Pryor's concept map (Figure 4.11) gives a picture of the dilemma he was trying to resolve—an approach that relied on rote learning versus the argument that Novak and Gowin (1984) make for the

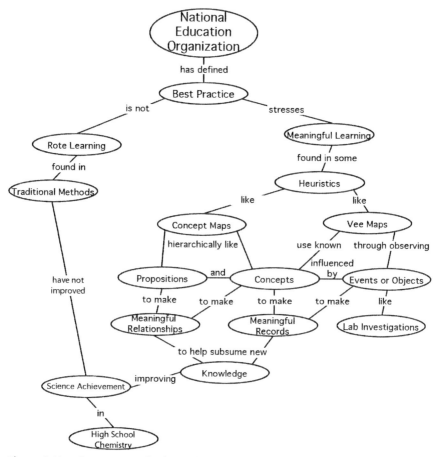

Figure 4.11. Concept map for improving high school chemistry.

value of meaningful learning guided by the heuristics of concept maps and Vees. Chris worked with his high school chemistry students guided by his concept map. The concept map then became the key concepts in the lower left of his conceptual framework in the Vee. The principles he tested appear in the concept map, guide the conceptual framework, and give support for the data he collected to answer the telling question, "Does the use of concept maps and Vee diagrams improve achievement in high school chemistry?" The results of his study, summarized in the right side of the Vee (Figure 4.12) offer support for the value of Novak and Gowin's heuristic tools to improve achievement. The elegance of concept maps and Vees is that Chris' entire study can be summarized dramatically in two figures.

Research Question: Does the use of Concept Maps and Vee Diagrams improve achievement in High School Chemistry?

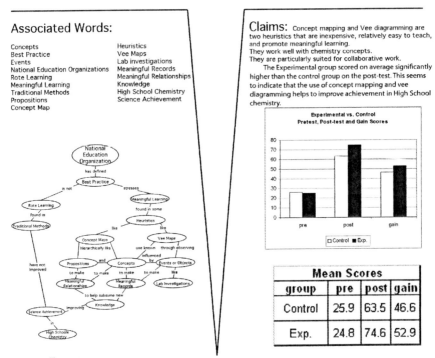

Associated Words:

Concepts	Heuristics
Best Practice	Vee Maps
Events	Lab investigations
National Education Organizations	Meaningful Records
Rote Learning	Meaningful Relationships
Meaningful Learning	Knowledge
Traditional Methods	High School Chemistry
Propositions	Science Achievement
Concept Map	

Claims:
Concept mapping and Vee diagramming are two heuristics that are inexpensive, relatively easy to teach, and promote meaningful learning.

They work well with chemistry concepts.

They are particularly suited for collaborative work.

The Experimental group scored on average significantly higher than the control group on the post-test. This seems to indicate that the use of concept mapping and vee diagramming helps to improve achievement in High School chemistry.

Experimental vs. Control Pretest, Post-test and Gain Scores

Mean Scores			
group	pre	post	gain
Control	25.9	63.5	46.6
Exp.	24.8	74.6	52.9

Event: Use a 2 group, pretest, post test design. The Experimental group will be required to use and construct Concept maps and Vee Diagrams. The control group will not use the heuristics. Scores on the tests will be compared

Figure 4.12. Vee for improving high school chemistry.

Improving High School Chemistry: Concept Maps and Vee Diagrams
Hugh C. Pryor
Abstract

This thesis describes use of concept maps and Vee diagrams as instructional tools for high school chemistry. Concept mapping requires learners to draw relationships among concepts in a meaningful network. Vee diagrams help students understand the structure and process of knowledge construction. Compared to a traditional curriculum approach, these heuristics facilitated higher achievement. The usefulness of these heuristics to meet the recommended standards of teaching and learning in science across the curriculum is emphasized. (Pryor 1995)

The Vee, Figure 4.12 answers the focus question about the use of concept maps and Vees to improve high school chemistry.

The examples in this chapter show that students can apply these heuristics in various disciplines. I see this as key to authentic educating. It is possible to teach elementary through graduate students to think at the highest levels (theoretical and value judgment) and apply these tools to evaluating their own lives—something that I develop further in subsequent chapters.

Chapter Five

Authenticity in the Classroom: From Literature to One-Act Plays and Personal Journals

After introducing educational theory relevant to this perspective, and explaining the heuristic tools, the next step is to show the results of authentic educating in the classroom. Maxine Greene (1988), a well-known authority on using literature in education—who was very encouraging after reading a previous draft of this text—exhorts teachers to educate students for empowerment. D.B. Gowin (1981) claimed that the aim of educating is to help learners change the meaning of their experience and become self-educating writers of their own life scripts. Clearly, philosophy and literature should be sources from which to generate authentic educating, and help students to move toward authenticity.

In this chapter, I discuss several novels to help define authenticity and offer techniques to enhance students' authenticity. Concept maps can help explicate literary works and students' personal lives. The concept of authenticity can focus these novels and lead students to better understanding of philosophy, literature, educating, and themselves.

The techniques have been used successfully in elementary through graduate school. Samples of student drawn concept maps about literary works, reaction papers—personal responses to readings—personal journals about issues of authenticity in students' lives, and concept maps showing these issues are shown. The aim of these writing assignments is to help students to understand the literary works. The self-selected personal development projects help them apply understanding of literature and philosophy to their lives.

As shown in Chapter 1, authenticity can be summarized in a concept map (Figure 5.1). The key concept: authenticity at the top is connected to subordinate key concepts by lines and words. The hierarchical network is created by identifying key concepts and then arranging them from most general at the

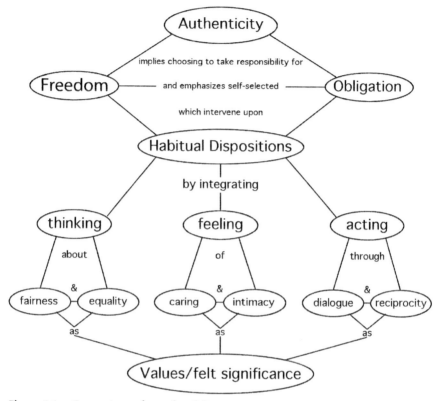

Figure 5.1. Concept map for authenticity.

top—those of equal importance and inclusiveness on the same horizontal—to the most specific at the bottom. There is fluidity to the concept arrangement, and any section of a map could be expanded with additional related concepts.

A major value of a map is that it externalizes thinking. One can rethink ideas by physically moving and rearranging key concepts into more meaningful patterns. Often students remark that the movement from a random collection of key concepts (e.g. ideas, thoughts, images, symbols, etc.) in their head, to rough sketches, to subsequently refined drawings is a powerful thinking experience, which allows a private and unobservable process to become organized and externalized.

The above concept map emphasizes the choice character of authenticity. Obligations develop through choice. Individuals need to act with the understanding that they have freedom to select their obligations, but choices affect one's habits, the person one is day to day. For example, if one chooses to be involved in a local musical or theatre group, one's daily habits will change. Rehearsal times require commitments that entail punctuality, but also, practice on one's own. Once one makes the choice to participate in a performance group, one's thinking, feeling, and acting are affected. Lines need to be read and memorized, or songs need to be practiced, other relationships are affected, and habits are changed. In this simple example, it is easy to see that by integrating one's thinking and feeling about this commitment, a person is able to act on values and take responsibility for freedom and obligations, thus creating ethical relationships that generate mutual reciprocity. One agrees to a time schedule, material to learn, a performance to attend, and a skill level to attain.

IN SEARCH OF AUTHENTIC CHARACTERS

The abstract concept of authenticity becomes concrete when applied to literary characters. When students understand characters from the perspective of authenticity, they can learn to integrate authenticity into their own lives. The following example shows the concept map of authenticity applied to Camus' character Meursault in *The Stranger* (1946). Meursault is a counter-example. As an anti-hero, he shows what authenticity is not.

Meursault in *The Stranger*

Camus' novel is an account of a French Algerian clerk who, through a bizarre set of circumstances, kills an Arab for no apparent reason—beyond that the sun was in his eyes. During the subsequent trial, when asked about how he felt about killing the Arab, Meursault tells the court that he lost interest in noting his feelings when he realized that life ends in death. He explained that since everyone dies in the end, life is meaningless. One life is as good as the next, but all are worthless. Basically, he has no feelings about the Arab's death or his own. Finally, he is condemned to death, primarily because of his indifference to the killing and that he showed no remorse for the murder.

While he is in jail awaiting execution, he begins to reconsider his life. He realizes that sensual pleasures dominated his life. For example, his affair with Marie aroused sexual impulses, but never amounted to love. In fact, he told her that love was a meaningless word. His philosophy of indifference seems justified as he passes his time in jail, the lack of cigarettes his biggest concern.

Only near the end of his life, when a priest comes to hear his last confession, does Meursault express emotion. He becomes angry with the priest and demands to be left alone. Afterwards, lying on the bed in his cell, he contemplates how he lived his life. Washed clean of anger toward the priest, he considers that if he had the chance, he would live his life as he did. Meursault seems to believe indifference is the appropriate reaction on the last page of the novel, a suggestion by Camus that Meursault has an ambiguous connection to the world and himself.

The issue of authenticity arises with regard to Meursault's life toward the end of the novel, as he contemplates the finality of the guillotine. The book ends with an ambiguous wish that those witnessing the execution hate him for committing the murder. But Meursault is not telling others what they *ought* to do; it seems merely his preference that his execution for murder be met with hate from others. Somehow, he seems to believe it appropriate that a large crowd of spectators *not* share his indifference. He wants to be greeted with hate. Again, Camus offers a term of endearment and a reaction of hostility—an ironic twist. In this way, Camus draws our attention to the importance of emotion.

At the end, is Meurault's indifference to murdering the Arab transformed into a wish to be hated for the murder he committed? Or is he suddenly convinced that emotion is key to making life meaningful? In subsequent books, such as *The Plague* (1972), *The Myth of Sisyphus* (1955), and *Resistance Rebellion and Death* (1961), Camus develops the theme of passionate commitment to rebellion in solidarity with others. Meursault's wish to be hated at his execution offers questions to be considered about the meaning of emotions in guiding one's life. These questions are key to discussion about authenticity that aims to integrate thinking and feeling into authentic action. Authenticity entails that one care about oneself and others. Meursault's indifference prevents movement toward authenticity (Figure 5.2).

At the end of his life, still in the process of appealing his death penalty, Meursault begins to integrate his previously detached thoughts with feelings he could not ignore. Pressured by imminent death, Meursault's catharsis of anger toward the priest—supplied by the courts to minister to his spiritual needs—helped him experience a sense of life's value, but Camus ends the novel with Meursault lacking authentic integration, with Meursault contemplating an indifferent world.

Thought without feeling leaves one isolated and alone. This suggests limitations to Kohlberg's cognitive theory of moral development and emphasizes the importance of an ethic of connection and caring—ideas advocated by Greene (1988), Gilligan (1982) and Noddings (1984). But it is a flourishing integration of thinking and feeling that characterizes authenticity. Meursault offers an excellent example of the disastrous consequences when one fails at this integration.

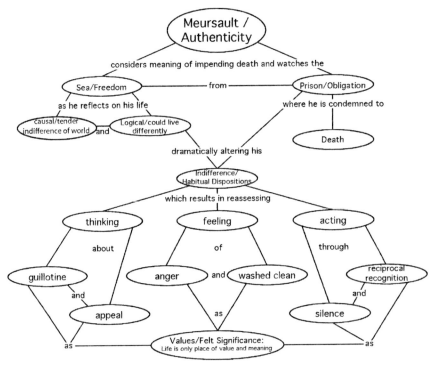

Figure 5.2. Concept map for *The Stranger*.

Edna in *The Awakening*

Another character who fails in her struggle with authentic integration is Edna in Kate Chopin's *The Awakening* (1981) that was set around the end of the Nineteenth Century. Maxine Greene said in her assessment of Edna in *The Awakening*, "Like so many women of her time, she has let herself be victimized by what she has taken for granted 'through habit' as natural, as given" (1988, 63). In the end, Edna committed suicide by drowning because she was unable to see an alternative. Several students, like many critics, blamed the ending on "society"—conventions which worked against women of the 1890s. Figure 5.3 shows that Edna does not move toward authenticity through suicide.

A sympathetic critic Priscilla Allen said "Divorce is not a consideration for in the 1890s this right had not been recognized generally or won" (Diamond and Edward 1988, 235). Allen described Edna's dilemma as "heroism," because "she is able to pursue her felt needs with so little guilt and that rather than settling for less than a chance to fulfill them she chooses instead to die

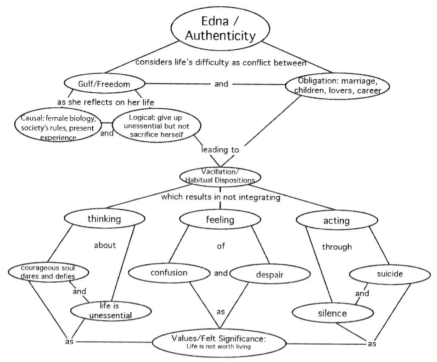

Figure 5.3. Concept map the *The Awakening*.

... it is a portrait of a woman determined to have full integrity, full person-hood—or nothing" (238).

Greene's account that Edna allowed herself to be "victimized," because she did not overcome her "habitual dispositions" seems more accurate. Edna could have chosen another plan. For example, she could have lived within the controversy and turmoil her author endured, which is a point of dispute among critics that could lead to fruitful classroom discussion.

STUDENTS RESPOND TO LITERATURE

For students, responding to *The Awakening* (1981) and *The Optimist's Daughter* (1978) was an opportunity to consider how two women struggled with issues of authenticity. The following is a concept map, then an excerpt from a student's reaction paper for *The Awakening* (Figure 5.4).

Belinda wrote in her reaction paper that, "the novel has a sensuous story line that tells of a woman's abandonment of her family and her secret

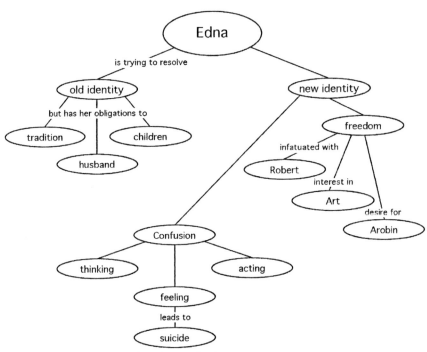

Figure 5.4. Concept map for *The Awakening*.

passionate desires which lead her to lose both her mind and eventually her life." She suggested that Edna's death was a result of confusion over priorities, i.e. the choice of death over struggle. From the viewpoint of authenticity, it is a result of her failing to do the hard work of confronting her freedom and obligations and make changes in her life.

In contrast, in Eudora Welty's *The Optimist's Daughter*, Laurel must confront her father's death and resolve a new direction for her life that integrates loss of her mother, husband, and father.

Belinda said about her concept map (Figure 5.5):

> Throughout the novel we see through Laurel's eyes her search for authenticity. *The Optimist's Daughter* is the story of a young woman who left her small hometown in Mississippi for Chicago and now returns home to help her dying father. After his death, alone in the house where she grew up, Laurel finally comes to an understanding of the past, herself, and her parents.

These concept maps demonstrate the student's ability to consider characters from the philosophic perspective of authenticity, and to apply concept

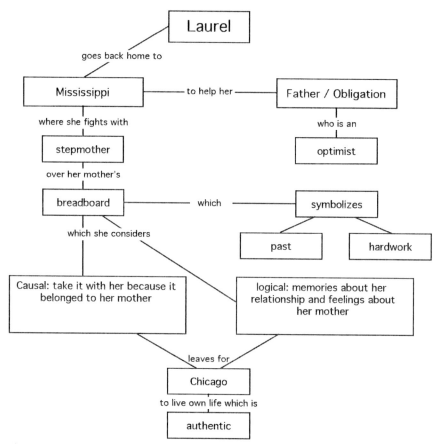

Figure 5.5. Concept map for *The Optimist's Daughter*.

mapping skills to literary assessment of the novels. The maps help them identify plots, themes, symbols, characters, motives, etc. The linking of abstract
concepts with literary analysis helps to integrate the two and expand the students' comprehension of both. But the next step toward enhancing students'
experience is to connect their academic work to their own lives.

THE SEARCH FOR AUTHENTIC
CHARACTERS CONTINUES

Zora Neale Hurston's *Their Eyes Were Watching God* (1990), Maya Angelou's *I Know Why the Caged Bird Sings* (1993), and Terry McMillan's
Waiting to Exhale (1992) can be considered stories of African-American

women in search of their own voice. As the female protagonists search for their own voice, the aim of their search allows one to ask the question whether an ethic of authenticity can help them answer the philosophic question, "What is the good life?"

Janie in *Their Eyes Were Watching God*

Zora Neale Hurston's *Their Eyes Were Watching God* describes Janie, a forty year old black women returning to her home town to tell her story in powerful dialect to a younger friend, Pheoby. Hurston identifies Janie's quest as a journey to explore the world and its people.

The image of an odyssey that Janie undertakes allows for discussion of these novels within the context of authenticity. Since Hurston's work is the earliest chronologically, and offered inspiration to several of the other authors, it establishes a launching point. As Virginia Woolf said, "A woman writing thinks back through her mother" (Woolf 1989, 101). Hurston is a powerful force in that matriarchal lineage, with significant connection to Alice Walker and Nobel Prize winner Toni Morrison.

Janie is married by arrangement between her grandmother—who raised Janie after her mother abandoned her—to a respectable local farmer Logan Killicks. But within a short time after the marriage, Janie's grandmother died. Within a year, Janie's dissatisfaction with the constraints of her arranged marriage led her to consider leaving with the handsome and exciting Joe Starks. Hesitant at first, Janie's conflict is between her grandmother's insistence on a safe marriage and the intrigue of Starks. Impulsively, she leaves Killicks and marries Starks, who eventually becomes mayor and successful store owner in a new town in central Florida built exclusively by African-Americans.

He is possessive and controlling of her as his wife. One day, after seven years of marriage, when she is twenty-four, he hits her. The incident makes her realize that she had thoughts and emotions that she did not share with him. In Rousseau's terms, it is the beginning of an "inner voice." This awareness allows her to understand those things that are essential and those that are peripheral.

She endures the abuse for another eleven years, but at thirty-five, she closed herself from him emotionally. Eventually Starks becomes sick and dies, leaving her financially secure. Finally, she begins a deliberate search for the horizon and acknowledges that she lived the way her grandmother insisted, but needed to go on with life as she wished. She moved beyond a life defined by her grandmother—through experience as a slave—and toward a sense of what was genuinely important to her.

Soon after, she meets then marries Tea Cake, a handsome twenty-five year old who treats her with respect. He talks her into moving to the Everglades to live. It is there that that she begins to find her own voice and live and act among people as she wanted. In the Everglades she is the social equal of those living there. Her relationship with Tea Cake allows her to achieve intimacy, which was missing in her previous two marriages. These are central issues in development of authenticity.

But her relationship with Tea Cake ends tragically. During a hurricane, a rabid dog bites Tea Cake and Janie must kill him in self-defense when he attacks her. But at the end of the story, she demonstrates her movement toward authenticity. She tells her friend Pheoby that she is satisfied to be back home and she understands how her life has changed. Further reflecting on her experience of love she says that it is dynamic and different for everyone.

Pheoby responds that the story has had great affect on her, but Janie explains about the necessity of genuine experience, that one must live one's own life to truly understand it. When Janie finishes they sit in silence. Afterwards Janie goes upstairs to her room alone. She realizes Tea Cake's memory is with her as the book ends and her life filled with experiences of her own making completes her understanding of herself and the world.

As Henry Louis Gates writes in the "Afterword" of the novel, Janie's upward mobility with her first two husbands was at the expense of her own personal development. But through experience in the social and intimate sphere, she moved toward authenticity. Through her character Janie, Hurston established the foundation for other black women writers to build upon. Gates emphasizes that Walker and Hurston helped to construct a positive view of black people.

The following reaction paper to Zora Neale Hurston's *Their Eyes Were Watching God* comes from a married student. Liz demonstrates insight into literature and authenticity to change the meaning of experience, which she described in her journal and concept map about an issue of authenticity in her life that appears in the next section. But in this reaction paper she identifies Janie's struggles. It is important for white students to read African-American women writers to understand these cultural differences.

Reaction Paper:
Zora Neale Hurston's Their Eyes Were Watching God

I enjoyed this book, especially the dialectic language. But I also enjoyed Janie's development from a young girl naively dreaming about love and marriage under a blooming pear tree, into a mature woman who knows her feelings and how to follow them.

Janie's search, I think, is for people, and for understanding of the world and her relationship to it: the "far horizon". Hurston writes "she had been getting ready for her great journey to the far horizons in search of people . . . But she had been whipped like a cur dog, and run off down a back road after things" (Hurston 1990, 85).

Men in search of power and things were what Janie found in her first two husbands, neither of whom I feel she really chose. Her first marriage, to Killicks, was an arranged marriage that Janie was more or less shamed into. He seemed to see Janie as an asset to his farm and as a means of personal comfort.

When Janie ran from this marriage, Starks presented himself as a promising opportunity. Some could argue that Janie chose to marry Starks, but I feel that her choice was more of running from than running to. In Starks, Janie found a man even more obsessed with power and things than her first husband. Starks' vision of Jane was that she be a great lady. Insisting on this role for her, he isolated her from the people surrounding her. She in turn isolated herself from him, and her repression and isolation were nearly complete.

When Starks dies, however, Janie seizes the opportunity to live. She says, "Ah done lived grandma's way, now Ah means tuh live mine" (108). In Tea Cake she finds a man who accepts her as a person, not an asset, and not some illusionary lady creature. Through intimacy of acceptance and Pheoby's friendship that allows dialogue and reflection, Janie comes to an understanding of "far horizons".

The insights she shares in her reaction paper are clearly articulated in her concept map about Janie (Figure 5.6). Liz sees Janie's conflict as overcoming the power that other people have over her life. Janie's struggle is to overcome ideas that her grandmother imposed upon her by arranging a marriage with a local farmer, Killicks, and then another repressive marriage to an ambitious businessman, Starks. Janie's journey in the novel is toward dialogue and intimacy with Tea Cake and her friend Pheoby, as Janie seeks knowledge of the world and herself, aiming her toward authenticity.

Ritie in *I Know Why the Caged Bird Sings*

In another story of movement toward authenticity, Maya Angelou develops Ritie, a young black girl raised by her grandmother who runs a grocery store in Arkansas, in the novel *I Know Why the Caged Bird Sings* (1993). Ritie is a girl suffering from failure of *reciprocal recognition*, a girl who wants to be white, with long blond hair and blue eyes. It is only "a cruel fairy stepmother . . . jealous of my beauty . . . turned me into a too-big Negro girl, with nappy black hair, broad feet and a space between her teeth" (2). Whites maintain a significant presence in this and the other novels, through failure of *reciprocal*

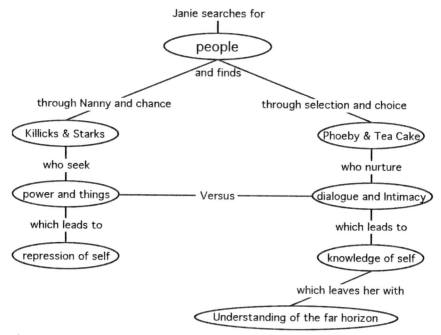

Figure 5.6.   Concept map for *Their Eyes Were Watching God.*

recognition. This failure of recognition is oppressive in this novel that takes place during the time when "Jim Crow" laws promoting segregation were in effect.

Similar to Janie, Ritie acknowledges the restraint from her grandmother's worldview "bordered on all sides with work, duty, religion and `her place'" (47). Like Janie, Ritie must construct her own world view from an identity based on rejection. Reflecting on being abandoned by her mother, she attributes her mother's beauty as the reason she did not want to raise children. It raises her question "what mother and daughter understand each other, or even have the sympathy for each other's lack of understanding?" (57).

But the unfairness of Whites to Blacks is made most palpable to her at graduation from eighth grade in 1940, at age twelve. As an invited speaker, Mr. Donleavy, a White man from the central school administration, talks about improvements to the local schools—the White school would get academic equipment and the Black school would get athletic facilities. To Ritie, this condemns her to the stereotype that Blacks cannot achieve academically.

She makes observations about what the world will be for her: "caught in the tripartite crossfire of masculine prejudice, white illogical hate and Black

lack of power" (231). In her mind there is no equal recognition, no principle of fairness "which demands equal chances for everyone to develop their own identity" (Taylor 1991, 50). Her identity in the intimate and social sphere is sacrificed. It is a tremendous challenge for her to develop an "inner voice" within the context of her situation. She must confront central and peripheral aspects of her identity given her awareness that: "It was brutal to be young and already trained to sit quietly and listen to charges brought against my color with no chance of defense" (Angelou 1993, 153).

Ritie says "Elouise, the daughter of the Baptist minister, recited 'Invictus' and I could have cried at the impertinence of 'I am the master of my fate, I am the captain of my soul'" (154). She continues a powerful description of loss of voice and then a regaining of her voice in the words of Patrick Henry "give me liberty or give me death" (156) as she sings the words of "Lift Ev'ry Voice and Sing" which she calls "the Negro national anthem" (155) conducted by a classmate. She regains her strength and recounts, "I was no longer simply a member of the proud graduating class of 1940; I was a proud member of the wonderful beautiful Negro race" (156). With this emotional commitment she attempts to establish a core to her identity.

Several years later, when she is fifteen she also worries about her sexuality and wonders if she may be a lesbian. Trying to prove to herself that she is not she finds a local friend and asks him to have sex with her. He does. Soon afterwards she finds that she is pregnant at sixteen.

She pretends that the pregnancy would have no consequences: "the first three months . . . were a hazy period . . . I didn't really link pregnancy to the possibility of my having a baby" (242). She avoids telling her mother, whom she knew was "violently opposed to abortions" (242). She says that she prided herself on not lying, but she acknowledges she was not beyond deceit. So, while living with her mother, she focused on "pretending to be that guileless schoolgirl who had nothing more wearying to think about than mid-term exams" (243). But as she approaches her sixth month of pregnancy, her mother leaves on business for a few months and Ritie says, "I felt treacherous allowing her to go without informing her that she was soon to be a grandmother" (244). After she gets her diploma during summer school, she leaves a note to her mother that she is pregnant, only three weeks before she is due. Her mother asks if she wants to marry the father; Ritie doesn't, and her mother agrees it is best not to. So Ritie has the baby.

Within the context of authenticity, Ritie's reactions indicate a resistance to acting upon the situation. She allows herself to be pregnant and abdicates responsibility. Ritie does not demonstrate authenticity, and one wonders what sort of caring connection she will be able to maintain with her baby. The social context of San Francisco in the late Nineteen Forties would be more

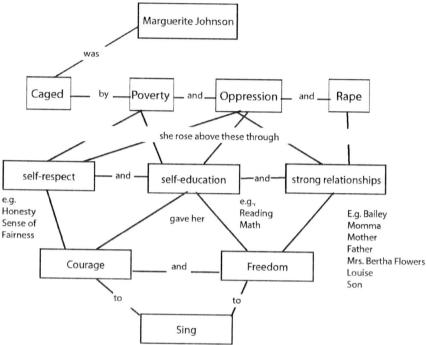

Figure 5.7. Concept map for *I Know Why the Caged Bird Sings*.

tolerant than that of her Arkansas childhood, but evidence of her inability to connect with others in the intimate sphere does not bode well for sustaining authentic relationships in the future. It is significant that the novel ends with the child's birth. But it is not difficult to imagine that she would soon abandon the child, and repeat the cycle initiated by her own mother. This could lead to significant discussion about authenticity.

Debbie, a graduate student, considers Ritie's situation in the above concept map (Figure 5.7) and in her reaction paper. For Debbie, that Ritie endures against abandonment and oppression counts as authenticity.

But, as Debbie says in her reaction paper,

> I concede that her apparent lack of intimacy and caring, as well as her actions to avoid dialogue and reciprocity are contrary to the stated definition of authenticity. And, maybe the fact that I know that Marguerite is Maya Angelou—one of the most-respected poets of our time—is interfering with my ability to judge the girl in the story based on how she behaved as a pregnant teenager (a hormone double-whammy). I think it's significant that her book, *I Know Why the Caged Bird Sings*, is sold not in the African-American Literature aisle. . . . but rather in the Poetry section. Reading her poetry inspired me to have her resolve to accept

events that impact our lives as opportunities to look harder at who we are and
decide what it is we want and need—and what we're willing to give to others.
She *is* authentic.

I would agree with Debbie that Ritie struggles against great disappointment
and isolation. She is certainly demonstrating courage and working to take
responsibility for her freedom. That Ritie eventually became Maya Angelou
says much about the struggle for authenticity. But it is on the far side of the
struggle, when one achieves responsibility for one's decisions and can engage
in intimate and reciprocal dialogue that one achieves authenticity. Great literature shows how hard the struggle is. Analyzing the struggle helps students
understand the concept and start to apply it to the script of their own life they
are writing. This is why a range of literature is so helpful in the classroom
from elementary through graduate school.

Savannah in *Waiting to Exhale*

Terry McMillan's *Waiting to Exhale* (1992)—that was made into a movie—is
about four contemporary African-American women. Set in the early 1990s in
the city of Phoenix, Arizona, it follows the lives of four educated women in
their mid-thirties—Savannah Jackson, Bernadine Harris, Robin Stokes, and
Gloria Matthews. Women in search of their identities through intimate relationships are major themes.

These African-American women have moved forward through education
and are with men who have moved into business to establish themselves with
the traditional American Dream. Savannah fits the tradition of Janie Crawford; hers is the life of the quest, and she ends up alone, while expanding
her relationship with the three other women. The men are reminiscent of Joe
Starks—in pursuit of money as power and control over women. But women
have their own careers.

Savannah's guidelines are to live a meaningful life through her career and
among friends and family. She has a college diploma and a job in Phoenix
with a television station. She has never been married, and at age thirty-six
her mother reminds her that being married is a key to a woman's life. But
the battle is more complex as Savannah explains because she agrees with her
mother that marriage is important, but she cannot let being unmarried ruin her
life. After several unsuccessful relationships, she concludes that it may not
happen and that her identity may not involve a man or children.

Savannah's mother insists the problem is that worrying about her career is
interfering with Savannah finding a husband. Savannah's mother emphasizes
her priorities, but does not have an example of success to show her daughter.

Savannah and her friends seem to repeat the lifestyle of their mothers and grandmothers early in their lives; but eventually, through their own effort achieve successful movement into their own lifestyle.

The following is my reaction paper, shared with students about *Waiting to Exhale*. Since I have students share reaction papers with each other in small groups, where students read to group members after distributing a copy of their reaction paper to each member, I find it worthwhile to share my reactions with the entire group sometimes. This gives the students a feel for what I am looking for in reaction papers and gives group members a chance to discuss issues of mutual interest.

Reaction Paper
Terry McMillan's Waiting to Exhale

> Bernadine gets a shop; Robin gets a baby; Gloria gets over a heart attack; Savannah gets over men. Things seem to change through this novel. I guess I feel good for Bernadine. Robin worries me. Gloria seems to deserve another chance. But it seems Savannah could continue the cycle that lures her to men who are not good for her, unless she learns to balance desire and intimacy.
>
> If Savannah truly does come to believe that she can make it on her own, then I believe she has moved in the right direction. I like the new job. I like that she is going to work with Bernadine's new beau about the Martin Luther King holiday, but she's out in the galleries looking. Maybe she will never move on. Maybe it's Bernadine to believe. But that is all in the future. The one I don't trust is Robin; she seems to use men and now has a baby. I wonder if she will be able to help the baby move into a more positive world view than she has. But she worries me.
>
> All in all, I hope the American Dream does not get out of balance. I'd like to see Savannah balance her career with her desires for a man, child, and even her smoking habit. She seems to be moving toward authenticity as she dumps Charles, dumps Kenneth, and is willing in the end to value her intimacy with Bernadine more that a date with a man. One can only hope that she learns to keep balanced on her movement toward authenticity.

Next is a concept map I sketched about Savannah Jackson for my reaction paper (Figure 5.8). The map shows concern about the balance Savannah needs in life to continue movement toward authenticity.

Looking at these characters, one can see the movement from living a script handed to them by their grandmothers or mothers and achieving their own authentic voice. Janie Crawford moved through several unsatisfying marriages to gain a greater sense of herself through her relationship with Tea Cake. Ritie Johnson gains a better sense of her self, but ends with the complications of a child at a young age. Savannah Jackson realizes that her

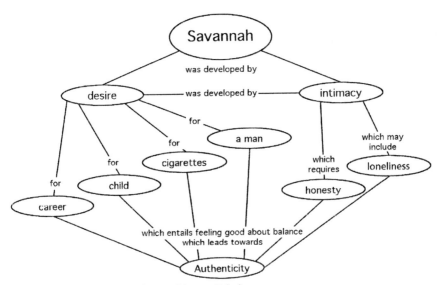

Figure 5.8. Concept map for *Waiting to Exhale*.

career and relationships together are what give meaning to her life. When she realizes that her need for a man and children is something that she can control, she achieves a significant move toward authenticity.

It is clear that growth toward authenticity requires experience upon which to reflect, and from which to make choices. In tandem with experience is access to education for these women because it leads on the practical level to opportunities for employment and financial independence from men—as Virginia Woolf said, a room of one's own and money are necessary.

Economic self-sufficiency is an issue in each of the novels. In capitalist America, money—and how one earns it—can be central to one's identity, as several characters demonstrate. The image of the American Dream that is part of Bernadine Harris' husband John's vision is misguided, as it is with Janie's husband Joe Starks' conflict between pursuit of money and power at the expense of reciprocity and intimacy because it destroys identities and marriages.

What is clear in these novels is women's movement from silence to voice—movement from lack of authenticity toward more authentic lives. These women connect to others with enhanced understanding of themselves and what they care about. American Dreams become engagement with American realities as Savannah Jackson indicates when she realizes that she will be happy when she acknowledges that living as a single woman can be a worthwhile life.

That attitude summarizes what Mayeroff stresses when he says:

> No one else can give me the meaning of my life; it is something I alone can make. The meaning is not something predetermined which simply unfolds; I help both to create it and to discover it, and this is a continuing process, not a once-and-for-all. (Mayeroff 1971, 62)

Connections between authenticity and caring are significant. These characters show movement toward authenticity and within the context of contemporary American democratic principles. The purpose of this chapter is to sketch what authenticity entails and to give examples of characters in contemporary American literature giving it voice.

STUDENTS CONSIDER THEIR AUTHENTICITY: PERSONAL JOURNALS AND CONCEPT MAPS

Authentic educating uses personal journals and concept maps with all students, elementary through graduate students, to help them move toward authenticity. This first example is from a fifth grade AESOP student's journal and a concept map that summarizes her authenticity issue (AESOP: Authentic Educating Summer Opportunity Program is an enrichment program that I have taught for gifted elementary students over the past ten years). These examples should give a feel for what is key to authentic educating. AESOP students maintained personal journals throughout the two-week session. They were able to keep their journals private, or share whatever they felt comfortable having me read. I explained that my aim in AESOP was to teach about philosophy and a theory of educating that aims to help them become better at learning, but also, to consider issues in their own lives that seemed to involve the issue of authenticity, similar to the issues we identified with characters in the novels we read. The following is a journal excerpt from a fifth grade student named Laura. Figure 5.9 is her concept map about her authenticity issue.

Journal Excerpt

> Some educators have what some people like to call "teacher's pets." I often wonder what are some qualities that teachers and professors like to find in a student. Do they like how the student dresses, or how they act, or maybe they go by first time impressions?
> My idea of a good educator is someone who treats all of his or her students fairly.
> Today we talked about fairness and people being equal. We also studied the word authentic. It means being true to your self. For the first time we went into

the computer lab. We started typing our concept maps about the story we were reading.

Last night, I woke up about 12 o'clock and I got a great idea of how to do my concept maps another way.

In her journal, she considers attributes of a good educator as someone who treats students fairly; and she considers the concept of authenticity, and how it applies to her life, how she can be true to her self. In the following concept map, she begins to assess the meaning of the education she wants. Her dilemma is whether she should continue in gifted education classes or regular education classes; in her map, she works through the various pros and cons of each.

The issue she was trying to resolve is an issue often discussed in the research about gifted children. She remained in the gifted program and returned to AESOP the following year as a sixth grader. Students have issues about choices they need to make about school or family. I see these as key to authentic educating for students in elementary through graduate school. Consider the following examples from students considering teaching as a career. Belinda was a business major considering elementary education as a major (Figure 5.10).

The students in the following examples were freshman through seniors in college. Many were making the transition from high school optimism to college realism about their future. Many expressed concern about choice of major,

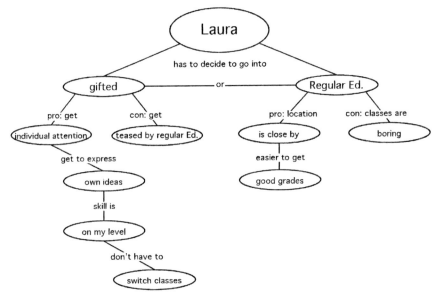

Figure 5.9. **Laura's concept map about her authenticity issue.**

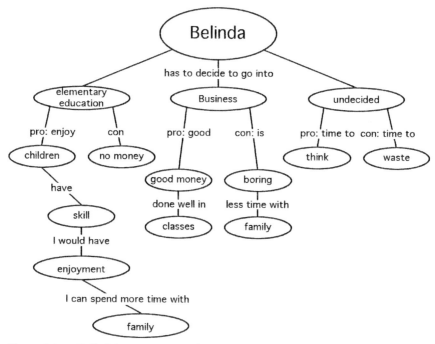

Figure 5.10.   Belinda's concept map about her authenticity issue.

and several about plans to transfer to another college. Each week the students shared their journals with me as the instructor, and at the end of the course they summarized their concerns and drew concept maps to explain their decisions.

Belinda's project involved choosing between a major in business or education. The conflict Belinda identified was between her feelings that teaching may be enjoyable, but that business offered the possibility for a more lucrative career. However, she believed teaching would allow her more time to share with her family, by which she meant eventually marrying and starting her own. The balance of the map tilts toward a need for a decision, but seemed to center on the "enjoyment" she perceived in teaching, versus business as "boring." The following semester she transferred from the business school into elementary education.

The next example is an excerpt from Alexis' journal and concept map (Figure 5.11) as she considered what area she wanted to teach.

Journal Excerpts

I have always wanted to be a teacher. Now that I am working on getting my education degree, I am trying to decide if I should teach Regular Education students or if I should get certified to teach Special Education students. There are many pros and cons to each option.

September 25—Today I went to observe in Mrs. H's K-1 Special Education class. Mrs. H has about eight students, each with a different disability or learning problem. In the beginning of the day they all come together for a group learning activity. Throughout the day the kids work on their own individual assignments, while Mrs. H works one on one with each of the students. I noticed that it requires a lot of effort and patience to keep the class in control. Most of the children had a very short attention span and had trouble staying on task. The teacher had to continually stop what she was doing to discipline her students.

October 19—Today I observed in Mrs. L's Regular Education class. Mrs. L has about 25 students. At the beginning of class she teaches the science lesson for the day and then she gives the students an individual or group assignment to work on. The students know exactly what they are supposed to be doing throughout the period. The class is very well behaved and Mrs. L doesn't have to spend very much time disciplining the students. The class is very organized and orderly.

I have had the opportunity to observe several classes since I have been at Stetson. I have learned a lot through my field observations and have had many good and bad experiences. I have been able to work one on one with many different students. I have also gotten the chance to observe in a Special Education class. I have discovered that it would be physically and mentally exhausting to teach Special Education students. From weighing out the pros and cons of each, I have decided that it would be much more practical for me to teach Regular Education students.

The final example is from Liz, who wrote the reaction paper and concept map for *Their Eyes Were Watching God*. Her ability to see her life in a new way because of her experience during the course is also powerfully described in this short excerpt from her journal.

Journal Excerpt

The experience of this course has been a beneficial one for me. Through it I have grown a little closer to understanding conflicts that until now I have struggled with without clarity or direction. It's helped me untangle strands of my life that have often seemed too complicated and painful to deal with. It hasn't solved my problems for me. That is something only I can do, and that will take time. But now I have a better sense of myself, of my conflict, and a vision of what that resolution should include.

Finally, the conflicts that she described in her journal during the course are graphically shown in her concept map (Figure 5.12). The conflict she

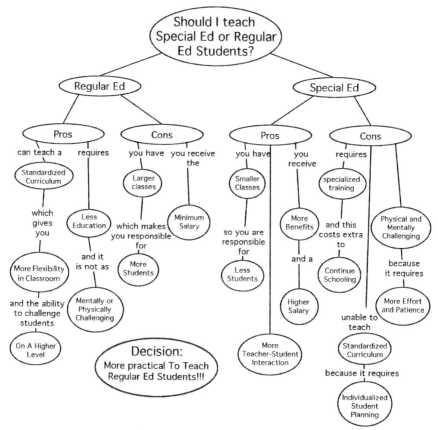

Figure 5.11. Alexis' concept map about her authenticity issue.

sees between commitments to her children and her own personal growth is juxtaposed with her sense of duty toward her husband.

The conflict she describes is one that has echoed in the voices of the literary characters under consideration, and speaks eloquently of Edna from *The Awakening* and Janie from *Their Eyes Were Watching God*. The aim toward authenticity for her is a journey that she acknowledges will take time. But it is a dramatic testament to the possibilities of developing authenticity through authentic educating.

It is apparent from the journal entries and concept maps that these students saw their experience differently during this course. Reading several outstanding novels gave them situations and characters to consider. The philosophic concept of authenticity gave them a way to reflect upon experience. The concept maps, reaction papers, and journals gave them new tools to assess literature and their own lives. Exploring these possibilities within the context of

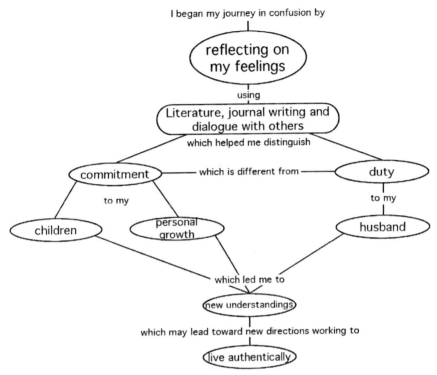

Figure 5.12.   Liz's concept map about her authenticity issue.

an academic environment offered students opportunities to apply classroom skills to personal growth.

Dewey, Gowin, Greene and many others emphasized educating that helps students to integrate thinking, feeling, and acting with an aim toward empowerment and self-educating. These techniques offer ways to implement this sort of educating—which students in the course valued. For example, Belinda said in her journal, "I enjoyed how we integrated philosophy, education, and literature together to determine authenticity."

The following is a short inventory to assess authenticity with a score sheet and interpretation of the results. It considers issues that appear in the concept map for authenticity and concerns students write about in their journals.

AUTHENTICITY INVENTORY

Record the number that most closely reflects your response to the following statements: 5 = strongly agree; 4 = agree; 3 = undecided; 2= disagree; 1= strongly disagree

1. We are born with purposes for our lives which we cannot change.
2. I have assessed my life goals significantly.
3. My actions reflect my beliefs.
4. My major goal in life is to live by my heart-felt choices.
5. Often I feel my life is out of control.
6. Moral choices are best judged by prescribed rules.
7. Often I do what my friends do, even it it's not what I want to do.
8. My choices define what is moral or immoral.
9. I have never assessed my religious beliefs.
10. I can explain my actions quite clearly.
11. Quality of life is best measured by quality of relationships.
12. I have developed a clear purpose for my life.

Self-Scoring Instructions

For items: 2, 3, 4, 8, 10, 11, 12, score 5 points for each answer marked SA; 4 for A; 3 for U; 2 for D; 1 for SD.

For items: 1, 5, 6, 7, 9, score 1 point for each answer marked SA; 2 for A; 3 for U; 4 for D; and 5 for SD.

Add the scores for all items. The sum is your Authenticity Score. The following chart summarizes the results:

51+ Above Average Movement Toward Authenticity
46-50 Average Movement Toward Authenticity
45- Less Than Average Movement Toward Authenticity

Interpreting the results

Above Average: Because you impose your own moral boundaries, rather than having them set by outside standards, you feel a great deal of responsibility for your decisions. You can usually explain why you act as you do. You develop close relationships, and issues like justice and equality are important for you in your interactions with others.

Average: You usually accept responsibility for your actions. You feel that, in most cases, you have the freedom to make your own decisions and you usually know why you act as you do.

Below Average: You often feel as if you are not in control of your own decision making, and generally do not accept responsibility for your actions. You may sometimes act by habit and not be able to explain your actions clearly.

Much is said about the need for classrooms to be places for active meaningful learning and writing across the curriculum. Concept maps, reaction papers, and journals are techniques to achieve these goals. They do not replace
the need for academic pieces; and students wrote formal academic papers to
develop those skills that are summarized in Chapter 6. A combination of techniques can promote intellectual and emotional growth that generates exciting
and worthwhile educating. Participating in one-act plays is another valuable
tool in authentic educating.

PARTICIPATING IN ONE-ACT PLAYS

Many students find participating in the one-act plays that summarize selected
novels as the most valuable aspect of authentic educating. During a play,
students summarize a piece of literature in a script that they act and a concept
map and Vee diagram that they present to an audience. Most students say
that it is a lot of work, but that they find it enjoyable and valuable for them to
better understand authentic educating and the concept of authenticity. Over
the years, I have worked with elementary students with a range of one-act
plays, including: *The Old Man and the Sea, The Cay, Harry Potter and the
Sorcerer's Stone*, etc. Following is a list of books I have used with elementary
students through graduate students. I make multiple copies of these books
available for students. I believe what students read should be negotiated between teacher and student.

Students read the novels, select fellow readers to participate in constructing
a concept map to summarize the novel, a Vee to answer the question "Does
the character move toward authenticity?" and a script based on the text to
summarize the plot. Students learn to construct maps and Vees in PowerPoint
and rehearse the script to perform in front of an audience. For the elementary
students in the AESOP program, the audience is parents and friends. The undergraduate students perform to the class. Recently, students videotape their play
around campus and edit their video, using various video-software on computers
with CD and DVD burning capabilities, and present the video in class on the
large screen. The recent plays—with the students responsible for directing and
editing—have improved the quality of the play and the students' experience.

Authentic Educating: Suggested Readings

Multiple copies of the novels in Table 5.1 are made available for students
to read, to concept map, or select as texts upon which to base the script of
one-act plays. Many other novels or literary works from Aeschylus to Shake-

Table 5.1. Suggested Reading List

Aesop's Fables (UG)	Aesop
I Know Why the Caged Bird Sings (UG)	Maya Angelou
The Wizard of Oz (UG)	L. Frank Baum
The Stranger (GS Project: HS French)	Albert Camus
The Awakening	Kate Chopin
The Little Prince (UG)	Antoine de Saint Exupery
The Great Gatsby	F. Scott Fitzgerald
One Child (UG)	Tory Hayden
The Old Man and the Sea (E, UG)	Ernest Hemingway
Siddhartha	Herman Hesse
Their Eyes Were Watching God	Zora Neale Hurston
A Portrait of the Artist as a Young Man	James Joyce
Waiting to Exhale	Terry McMillan
Winnie the Pooh (UG)	A.A. Milne
The Bluest Eye	Toni Morrison
Sula	Toni Morrison
Island of the Blue Dolphins (E, UG)	Scott O'Dell
Harry Potter and the Sorcerer's Stone (E)	J.K. Rowling
Oh, The Places You'll Go! (UG)	Dr. Seuss
The Giving Tree (UG)	Shel Silverstein
The Joy Luck Club (UG)	Amy Tan
The Kitchen God's Wife	Amy Tan
The Cay (E; UG)	Theodore Taylor
The Death of Ivan Ilyich	Leo Tolstoy
The Adventures of Huckleberry Finn (UG)	Mark Twain
Temple of My Familiar	Alice Walker
The Optimist's Daughter	Eudora Welty
Charlotte's Web (UG)	E.B. White
Stuart Little (UG)	E.B. White
The Velveteen Rabbit (UG)	Margery Williams
A Room of One's Own	Virginia Woolf

speare to Zola or contemporary writers can be selected. Plays performed by students are labeled: Elementary Students (E), High School (HS), Undergraduate Students (UG), Graduate Students (GS).

The following is a student essay about the experience of performing in a play and how it demonstrates authentic educating:

How Does The Play Experience Demonstrate Authentic Educating?

Throughout the course of the semester, I have continuously been exposed to a new theory in teaching: authentic educating. Upon completion of this class, I feel as though I have a greater understanding of the ideas and concepts that this theory encompasses and how we, as educators may want to implement them within our classrooms.

Perhaps the most important piece of work that has helped me truly understand its meaning is Dr. Robert Leahy's "Authenticity: From philosophic concept to literary character" (Leahy 1994). Within it we find two essential definitions of authenticity and authentic caring. As Dr. Leahy briefly sums up, "authenticity can be described as a personal attitude that aims toward taking responsibility for freedom and obligation; one's choices integrate reason and emotion through dialogue, reciprocal recognition, intimacy, and caring to construct one's self as a moral individual" (447). He also states, "Maybe genuine teaching—which implies helping others grow in formal and informal settings—is the best example I can offer of authentic caring" and later on " . . . we need to do more to make teaching of ethics central" (461).

One of the activities I had the opportunity to participate in during this class was the production of a play. Through it, I was able to actively incorporate the ideas behind authentic educating, including the philosophic perspectives of existentialism, which emphasizes personal meaning and responsibility and progressivism, which emphasizes democratic principles and reconstruction of experience. Rather than write a term paper, together four other girls and myself chose to produce *The Velveteen Rabbit*, a children's classic.

Perhaps one of the most important aspects of any project or lesson being taught is the personal meaning that the student can take from the experience and apply to his or her life afterwards. Existentialists most often believe that "schooling should be practical and provide children with sound instruction that prepares them to live life" (Parkay 1998, 90). During this assignment, not only did I learn a little about myself, but I also learned about other people and how I work with them. Often times, when I engage in group projects, I tend to take on the leadership role, essentially "the boss". This is probably one of my biggest weaknesses because I have certain ways of doing things, and if it's not going to be done my way, then I don't want others to do it at all. Because I was aware of this being one of my faults, throughout this project I tried to step back and participate on the same level as everyone else in my group. However, what I have learned through discussion with members of my team and through the actual experience is that it is essential that someone step up and take the leadership position. Otherwise, there is no one to hold the group responsible for the completion of requirements within the assignment. Sometimes, it becomes absolutely necessary for a leader to delegate jobs to members within the group so the work will be done efficiently and on time. Through this project, I've learned that it's ok to be the leader, as long are you are not "the boss". To be effective, it is essential to listen to others' ideas and incorporate them into the project so that everyone feels as though they are receiving equal treatment.

A second component of any group project is responsibility. Each group member must fully commit to the assignment and to his and her members on the team. I must say, that this was perhaps the best group I've ever worked with before. Each member of the group was equally concerned with contributing equivalent amounts of work. Most of the time, we worked on each of the assignments within the project together, allowing us to equally contribute our ideas and thoughts into the final product. However, we divided up other areas of the play as well, such as the costumes and props. Members were responsible for their characters' attire and items needed in their scene. By separating the tasks, we saved a tremendous amount of time, permitting us to do more run-throughs and perfect our acting.

Because I was working with other people, it was important to incorporate democratic principles into our group as well. By this, I mean we all had to work together in efforts to achieve a common goal, in this case, the final production of *The Velveteen Rabbit*. Each part of the play had to be carefully examined, including the dialogue, the concept map, the Vee diagram, the backdrops, and the props. As we viewed each section, it was important that each of us agree on the details of production to avoid conflict and encourage unity. Perhaps the only problem we ran into during the production of this play was in the early stages of planning. On two separate occasions, we set up meeting times in the library to get together to converse and organize the play. However, both times one of our members did not attend. Rather than simply eliminate her from the project, we confronted both the instructor and the individual to notify them of our concerns. Through this confrontation, we were able to work out the problem, eventually allowing the individual to do another assignment rather than the play.

The final concept we will discuss in Authentic Educating is the reconstruction of the experience. Although this state has not yet occurred, I'm almost positive it will some day down the road. In the future, I will be able to reflect upon my experiences of the play production and apply what I've learned from it to new group activities. I will be able to recall techniques that worked (communication, delegating duties), and perhaps recall methods that need improvement. Overall, the production of the play was a great experience. I met new people and made new friends. By incorporating concepts for Authentic Educating, I believe I am well on my way to becoming an authentic individual!

Melissa's essay summarizes key concepts about authenticity and shares an honest account of her issue regarding being "the boss" in previous group experiences. She demonstrates insight into what concerns she had about working with others, and how she dealt with them from the perspective of authentic educating. Of course, I have to be skeptical about students' enthusiasm for authentic educating during interviews, but I believe the girls were honest about how valuable they felt the experience was for them—you ought to see the video of the play and the interview.

The following evaluation chart allows group members to evaluate themselves and each other. Often, students are generous grading each other. But when there are difficulties with group members—like failure to attend meetings or fulfill obligations—this evaluation gives guidelines for students to assess each other. It emphasizes the importance of members working together and informing the instructor about potential conflicts, usually regarding incompatible schedules. Occasionally, cast members meet with me to help

Table 5.2. Play: Group Member Evaluation

Evaluator's Name:

Name of Play:

This is an evaluation for group members involved in performing a play. Enter the first
and last name of each group member in the column headings. Please record a letter
grade (A: excellent; B: good; C: fair; D: poor; F: failed) for each group member's
Overall Contribution (include yourself) to the preparation and performance of the play.
Next, assess each group member's participation in preparation and performance of the
play by recording a letter grade for the concepts from the map of authenticity.

Enter first and last names in column headings	Evaluator	Member	Member	Member	Member
Overall Contribution					
Authenticity					
Fairness					
Equality					
Caring					
Intimacy					
Dialogue					
Reciprocity					
Strengths: Please make comments where appropriate					
Suggestions for improvement: Please make comments where appropriate					

Please make suggestions to improve preparation and performance of plays:

distribute the work fairly, or to reassign students to other projects, such as a
term paper, done independently, instead of the group project.

REVIEW AND REFLECT

The following questions refer to the Authentic Educating: Suggested Readings:

1. Select a novel about an ethnic group other than your own. Read it and
   write a one-page reaction paper to it that you share with a group of two
   or three students.
2. Select a character from the novel you read, and in a well-constructed essay of approximately one thousand words, assess their movement toward
   authenticity.

Students performing The Wizard of Oz.

3. Describe how reading about a character from literature helped your own movement toward authenticity.
4. Construct a concept map that describes the major conflict a character undergoes in the novel you read.
5. Construct a concept map that identifies an issue of authenticity in your own life and develop a resolution using a personal journal.
6. Pose a question about *authentic educating*, and using Gowin's learning Vee attempt to answer it.
7. Select a novel from the list or suggest an alternative and with a group, produce a play.

Chapter Six

Panels, Presentations, Papers, and Projects

As I mentioned in the beginning of this book, authentic educating entails academic and personal projects. I believe that we should help students learn to read and write using efficient and effective tools. But we should help them to become better people also. Authentic educating entails a range of panels, papers, presentations, and projects. Panels require students to assess articles about an educational issue, summarize key concepts, answer the telling question, and respond to questions from a moderator and audience. Papers guided by concept maps and Vees require library and online research and writing and revisions. Presentations require students to organize ideas and summarize them forcefully and coherently in front of a group. Projects require students to do field research and produce results.

PANELS

Panel discussions give students an opportunity to teach. The ability to present material in an organized and interesting manner is a key to authentic educating, especially for students who want to become teachers. The maps and Vees in this section are based on articles in James Noll's *Taking Sides: Clashing Views on Controversial Educational Issues* (1999) used in an introductory education course comprised mostly of freshman and sophomores. The articles are selected by class vote. The first four to nominate and support an article become panel members, if a full class vote selects the article to be read. In sessions prior to beginning the panels, students work in the computer lab to develop their concept maps and Vees.

Panel discussions involve four students, divided into pairs representing opposite sides of a particular issue. The pair constructs the concept map and

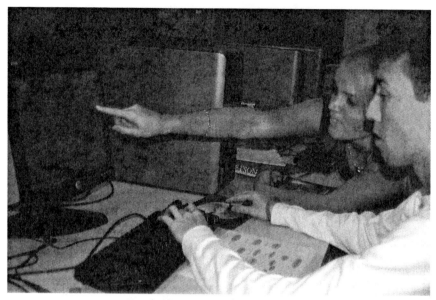

Panel preparation in the computer lab.

Vee to answer the question posed by the issue. Each student is given three to five minutes to present the map or Vee for their side. A concept map summarizes the article, and as students present they clarify the meaning of the concepts and explain how the concepts fit together. The student presenting the Vee explains how the concept map helps construct the answer to the telling question. Printed copies of the concept map and Vee are distributed to class members at the beginning of the presentations, so they can make notes during the presentation and have a record for future reference. After each of the four students present, they respond to questions from a moderator and the audience, comprised of class members. For the first few panels, I moderate. Afterwards, students who participated on a panel become moderators. The photo below shows the moderator at the far right and to her right are the four panel members. Everyone is watching embedded video of a panel member presenting the Vee diagram for one side. Afterwards, there is discussion and questions from the moderator and audience.

In this form of authentic educating, panel members summarize key concepts from a particular text, evaluate opposing arguments, and respond to questions. As moderators, students give feed back about the maps and Vees, ask panel members questions, and handle questions from class members and instructor addressed to panel members.

The following map and Vee (Figures 6.1 and 6.2) are from the "Yes" side of a panel considering the issue of compulsory education based on an article

Panel members presenting in the classroom.

by Horace Mann. Presenting the map, students start with the first concept at the top, explain it and then bring in each of the related concepts, so that the map appears on the screen one bubble and connecting line at a time and forms statements that become the principles in the Vee.

The Vee answers the telling question guiding this controversial issue, "Should school attendance be compelled?" (Figure 6.2). The answer, according the author Horace Mann is "Yes." The pair presenting his side assesses the answer using their concept map and Vee. The key quotes that they place in the right side of the Vee as "records" help to construct their knowledge and value claims that answer the question.

In this way, they learn to use technology to construct visual aids that they present to begin the panel. This is an opportunity for direct instruction. Afterwards, their presentation and ability to respond to questions is evaluated by the instructor and audience.

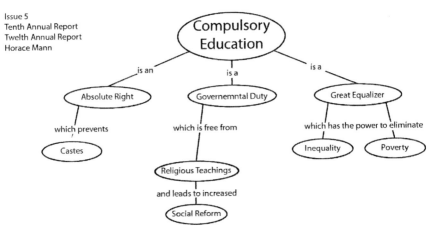

Figure 6.1.   Concept map for panel presentation about compulsory education.

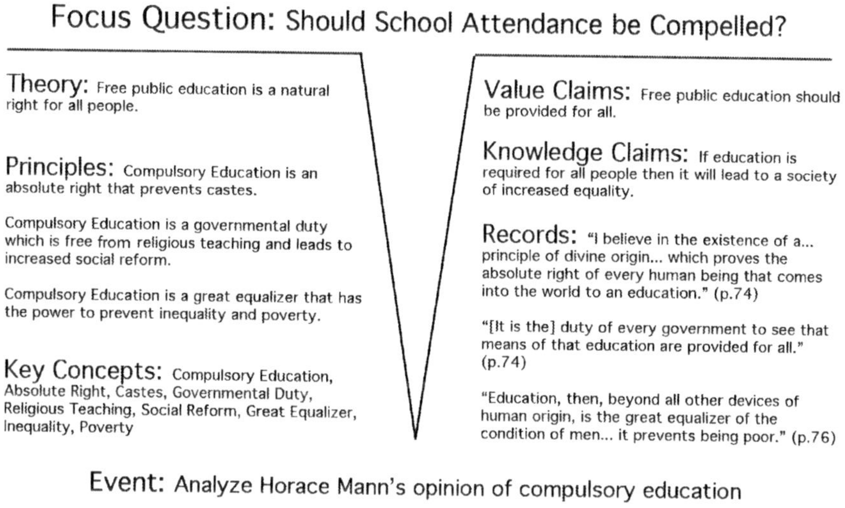

Focus Question: Should School Attendance be Compelled?

Theory: Free public education is a natural right for all people.

Principles: Compulsory Education is an absolute right that prevents castes.

Compulsory Education is a governmental duty which is free from religious teaching and leads to increased social reform.

Compulsory Education is a great equalizer that has the power to prevent inequality and poverty.

Key Concepts: Compulsory Education, Absolute Right, Castes, Governmental Duty, Religious Teaching, Social Reform, Great Equalizer, Inequality, Poverty

Value Claims: Free public education should be provided for all.

Knowledge Claims: If education is required for all people then it will lead to a society of increased equality.

Records: "I believe in the existence of a... principle of divine origin... which proves the absolute right of every human being that comes into the world to an education." (p.74)

"[It is the] duty of every government to see that means of that education are provided for all." (p.74)

"Education, then, beyond all other devices of human origin, is the great equalizer of the condition of men... it prevents being poor." (p.76)

Event: Analyze Horace Mann's opinion of compulsory education

Figure 6.2. Vee for panel presentation about compulsory education.

The map guides construction of the Vee. In the bottom left, the concepts from the map are listed in the Vee. The principles should be stated in the map and become the principles listed at the next level. In some cases, students use the principles to develop a theory about the answer to the question. In other cases, only principles are listed because the article does not develop a theory about the issue. The right side of the Vee requires excerpts from the text to support the claims on the left side.

The right side offers practical answers to the question through support from the text. The knowledge claim is a factual statement about the answer to the question. The value claim is a statement that suggests something is good, ought to be done, because it is better than the alternatives. In this way, students learn to separate fact from value. They get a better understanding about how to construct an argument and support their viewpoint at the highest levels of human thinking using practical tools that move them to the highest levels of Bloom's Taxonomy. Also, they get experience presenting in front of an audience.

Presenting the Vee, the question is first at the top, then the event at the bottom—what students did to answer the question—is presented next. The key concepts are shown, and the principles restated from the map, and the theory can be introduced. Going to the right side of the Vee, the presenter identifies quotes from the text to support the conceptual side on the left. Then, the knowledge claims are presented and finally the value claims, which support the theory on the left.

Table 6.1. Panel Presentation Evaluation

Presenter:

Letter Grade:

	Excellent: A	Good: B	Fair: C	Poor: D	
Concept map or Vee					Disorganized
Well poised					Hesitant
Clearly knowledgeable					Uncertain
Dynamic delivery					Occasional lapses
Emphasized key points					No key points
Voice modulation					Difficult to hear
Eye contact					Avoided audience
Use of notes					Read continuously
Reference to text					No text reference
Articulate answers					Vague responses

Strengths:

Suggestions for improvement:

Panel members are evaluated anonymously by students in the class and graded by the instructor with the evaluation form above. The student evaluations are returned to the presenters at the end of the session and I return my evaluation the next session. Each category is worth ten percent and averaged for an overall score. The panels are videotaped. Students are able to edit the video tape to insert video into their PowerPoint and select clips during the discussion to add to the presentation and keep the embedded video for professional portfolios and to discuss with the instructor. In this way, they get immediate feedback from peers, evaluation by the instructor, and the opportunity to edit video to assess what others have seen. Since each student is able to participate in two panels, there is often dramatic improvement in the second presentation based on what they learn from the first. The opportunity to see themselves as others see them and reflect upon their experience is a powerful tool.

PRESENTATIONS

Panel presentations are in a structured and timed format. But students can present concept maps and Vees about projects they are doing, fiction and nonfiction books they are reading, or plays they are planning or have performed.

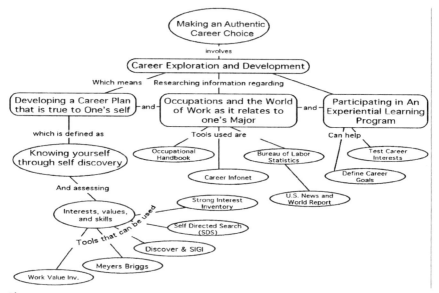

Figure 6.3. Concept map about making authentic career choices.

The next concept map (Figure 6.3) summarizes a graduate student's project. As a career counselor in the business school pursuing a Master's degree in education, Ann Marie applied principles of authentic educating to a course she was developing to teach undergraduates about making career choices. Her concept map was part of her PowerPoint presentation and discussion about her semester project, developed in conjunction with the assistant dean in the business school, to enhance career counseling for undergraduate business majors. The key steps are using self-assessment tools, learning about careers, and getting experience through internships. Eventually Ann Marie used the map to guide her Master's thesis.

Figures 6.4 and 6.5 were done by a freshman undergraduate for a presentation about the Russian Revolution in his history class. The map and Vee together help to answer the telling question "What were the causes and outcomes of the Russian Revolution?" Presentations of this sort require several hours to read the original sources and several hours to construct and reconstruct the map and Vees in PowerPoint.

Students report that the heuristics help them comprehend the reading so that they are better able to explain it to others. Generally, they agree that the map is the easier of the two heuristics to use, but that the Vee gives them a comprehensive view of material. Thomas identifies three major factors that he expands in the map in order to answer the telling question in the Vee.

Figure 6.4.   Concept map about the Russian Revolution.

Focus Question: What were the causes and outcomes of the Russian Revolutions?

Theory: The Russian Revolution resulted from the importency of the tsar and the provincial government culminating in Bolshevik controlled Russia.

Principles: 1) Tsar Nicolas II reactionary, oppressive and apathetic attitude caused social and economic turmoil. 2) The February Revolution was spawned because of the tsar's actions. However their own incompetence by appointing Trotsky and launching a new offensive in WWI led to the October Revolution. 3) The October Revolution was a Bolshevik Revolution. The Bolshevik's inability to unify Russia and control the villages and rural areas led them to civil war. 4) Civil War between Bolsheviks and ex-tsarist, France, England, Japan, and E. European nationalists ends with a Red victory by further devastates the nations economy. However, it establishes Lenin and the Bolsheviks control over Russia.

Key Concepts: Russian Revolution, Tsar Nicholas II, Impotent, Reactionary, Oppressive, Old Regime, Apathy, Social Unrest, Unstable Economy, February Revolution, Liberals/ Nationalists, Impotence, WWI, Trotsky, Revolution, October Revolution, Bolshevik Revolution, Villages, Rurual Areas, Civil War, Red's Victory, Lenin

Value Claim: The Provisional Government and the Tsar should have been overthrown because they were to reactionary and incompetent.

Knowledge Claim: Impotency from the tsar and the Provisional Government forced the October revolution and the Red/White civil war further devastated the Russian economy.

Records: 1) in 1912 Tsar Nicholas II massacred 200 striking miners (Read 34). Wages only increased by 50% while all products cost increased by 100-500% (Read 41). 2) On Sept. 25 Trotsky, a radical Bolshevik, was elected to head of the army (Read 57-58). The Provincial Government lost army support because they were reluctant to side with a government which was trying to embroil them in fighting with the Germans (Read 59). 3) Lenin argued that the peasantry would be the rural equivalence of the proletariat. Lenin was wrong and the rural economy is flung into deeper crisis (Read 226-227). Ex-tsarist mostly consisted of confused and conservative peasants (Read 194). 4) Total decrease in output after civil war-finished products 16%, mining 29%, oil 36%, metal 10%, wool 34% (Read 192).

Event: The Russian Revolutions

Figure 6.5.   Vee about the Russian Revolution.

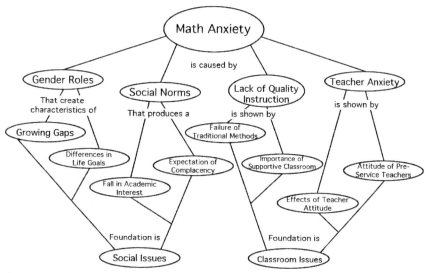

Figure 6.6. Concept map about math anxiety.

Figures 6.6 and 6.7 are from the presentation of a senior about a research study he conducted during the semester. At the beginning of the semester, students are required to develop a question that will guide their research. During the course of the semester, as they conduct library research, research through ERIC (Education Resources Information Center) and various online sources, such as *Google*, they refine the question and develop a concept map

Focus Question: What causes math anxiety?

Theory: There are causes and remediation for math anxiety.

Principles:

- Math anxiety is a result from gender stereotypes.

- Math anxiety is developed through society standards and attitude toward math.

- Traditional lecture setting in intermediate elementary is a major cause of math anxiety.

-Better instruction in content and methods for pre-service teachers in important for prevention.

Key concepts: math anxiety, gender roles, social norms, quality instruction, teacher anxiety, growing gaps, learning goals, academic interest, expectation of complacency, traditional methods, supportive classroom, teacher attitudes, pre-service teachers, social issues, classroom issues

Value Claims: The best way to remediate math anxiety is to prevent it, through better preparation in content and methods for pre-service teachers.

Knowledge Claims: Math anxiety will never fully be "cured," but there are many ways to lessen the effects it has on our students and society.

Records: "Boys are twice as likely to say they want to become scientists or engineers, but girls express a preference for professional, business, or managerial occupations (U.S. Department of Education, 1990)."

"Mathematics anxiety is so wide spread, many adults easily confess, 'I was never good in math,' as if displaying a badge of courage for enduring the hardship of the experience (Batista, 1999)."

"around fourth grade most teachers leave the world of concrete and tend to lean toward the abstract..... Most research shows that the forth grade is often when students first experience math anxiety (Lefingwell, 1999)."

"Though it may have serious consequences in both daily life and in work, mathematics anxiety has its roots in teaching, teachers, and has been tied to poor academic performances of students, as well as to the effectiveness of elementary teachers (Lindstrom, 1998)."

Event: Researching the causes and remediation of math anxiety

Figure 6.7. Vee about math anxiety.

and Vee. Toward the end of the semester, after completing a second draft of the paper that runs two to five thousand words, they present to members of the seminar. They distribute handouts with the map and Vee during a twenty minute presentation and question and answer period.

Ray's study was about math anxiety in the elementary school, during which he observed in local schools and interviewed students and teachers to answer his telling question.

Figure 6.8 is a concept map based on an article by Nick Colangelo from his *Handbook on Gifted Education* (1998). Alexis was doing an independent study on gifted education. Class projects and independent studies allow students to pursue personal interests in education. They also allow them to contact major figures in any field. With email so accessible, students can contact authors to get personal responses to their questions regarding the author's writing and their own motivating questions. Alexis was considering doing graduate work in gifted education. Reading Nick's handbook and corresponding with him gave her firsthand experience to assess her interest in the field and get to know people who are having affect on education nationally and internationally. As students pursue their interests they realize that getting to know influential people in the field helps them understand the issues and get a better feel for where they see themselves going. This is true for elementary through graduate students.

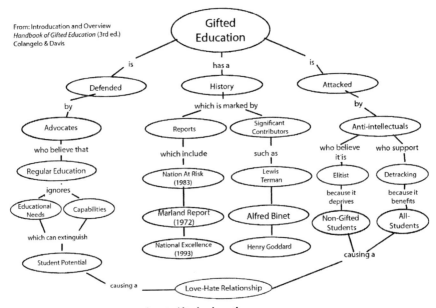

Figure 6.8.   Concept map about gifted education.

PAPERS AND PROJECTS

The presentations in the previous section were done in conjunction with papers students were writing and as stand alone pieces to summarize various research projects. This section summarizes several projects that undergraduate and graduate students implemented in local schools. The first describes an undergraduate student's project during her student internship at a local elementary school. A graduate student who teaches high school chemistry did the second project. The third was by a graduate student teaching a college level world music course. Excerpts from these projects show how teachers can use techniques in this book with their own students.

Project 1: Elementary School
Moving Toward Authenticity in the Whole Language Classroom
Amy Michelle Catt

Abstract

This article sketches connections between the whole language perspective, based on work by Goodman (1991) and the philosophic concept of authenticity, based on work by Taylor (1991) and Leahy (1994) for the elementary school classroom. The article uses the heuristic device of concept mapping, from Gowin's theory of educating (1981), to apply the concept of authenticity to works of children's literature: *Island of the Blue Dolphins* (1960) and *Charlotte's Web* (1952).

Authenticity in Charlotte's Web

Charlotte's Web has been popular among children for nearly half a century. The characters and plot are rich and full of enchantment, adventure and excitement. In relation to the ethic of authenticity and the philosophy of whole language, it is an exceptional curriculum selection. Using the concept map of authenticity, several characters can be analyzed to show how authenticity can enhance life.

Fern, the little girl who pleaded with her father to let Wilbur—the runt of the pig litter—live exhibits characteristics of authenticity. Fern chooses to save Wilbur and nurse him through infancy. Even though her father said it was customary to kill the weak runt of the litter, Fern felt this was not fair, and she was willing to make sacrifices to raise him. At two months of age, Wilbur, no longer a runt after Fern's nurturing, is sold to a neighbor, Mr. Zuckerman. Fern, upset at the loss of her friend, visits Wilbur nearly everyday. "It made her happy just to be near the pig, and it made Wilbur happy to know that she was sitting there, right outside his pen" (White 1952, 16). Because of Fern's affection and care for the pig, Wilbur grows to love her and their relationship becomes important. Because of White's personification of the animals it is possible for Fern and Wilbur to develop what Taylor (1991) calls reciprocal recognition, enhancing their lives through their relationship. Wilbur develops other authentic relationships as well. Charlotte, the gray spider, who lives in the doorway above Wilbur's pen, becomes a friend who "was to prove loyal and true to the very end" (41) and comes to Wilbur's rescue. Even though Fern saved Wilbur's life earlier, he faced danger again. Mr. Zuckerman planned to butcher Wilbur, but Charlotte was determined to keep him alive. She succeeds in saving his life by spinning messages about Wilbur into her web.

Charlotte does save Wilbur's life. In fact, he outlives her. However, Wilbur never forgets Charlotte, and he continues his devotion to her through pledges of loyalty and friendship to her children and grandchildren even though "none of the new spiders ever took the place of her in his heart" (184).

In contrast, Templeton, the rat, is inauthentic. He never bonds intimately with others. Templeton's philosophy of life is self-interested. "The rat had no morals, no conscience, no scruples, no consideration, no decency, no milk of rodent kindness, no compunctions, no higher feeling, no friendliness, no anything" (46). Templeton does things that appear to point in the direction that he thinks about others. However, when examined, his intentions are always self-centered.

The concept map, Figure 6.9, describes Charlotte's authenticity based on her relationship with Wilbur that led toward feelings of significance in her life. Discussions with students about the relationships among these concepts and characters can enhance students' understanding and movement toward authenticity. Concept maps done about characters that students feel were inauthentic, such as Templeton, extend dialogue and comprehension.

Authenticity in Island of the Blue Dolphins

Written by Scott O'Dell, the first American to win the Hans Christian Anderson Medal, *Island of the Blue Dolphins* (1960) is a powerful tale of nature and personal discovery. Based on the true story of an Indian girl, Karana, who in the early 1800s spends eighteen years alone on an island off the shore of California, it won a Newberry Medal.

Karana's movement toward authenticity is a slow and steady progression. Because of a battle with otter hunters, her tribe is decimated. Most warriors, including her father the chief, die in the battle. Kimki, the new chief, afraid the tribe will not survive, looks for new territory. Soon Kimki

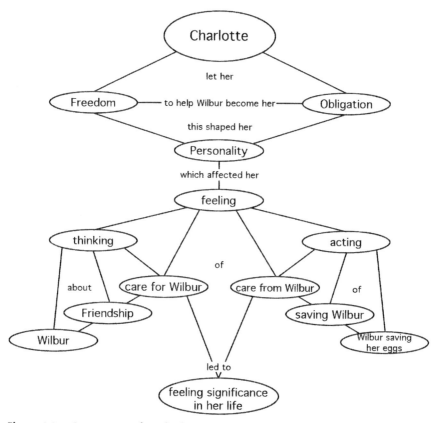

Figure 6.9. Concept map for *Charlotte's Web.*

sends a ship to bring the survivors to their new land. Karana jumps off the ship as it departs when she sees her brother left on shore. She felt it was her obligation to stay with him until another ship arrived. Several days after the ship set sail, Karana's brother is killed by wild dogs, and she is left with desire to revenge her brother's death. Vengeance becomes the driving force in her life.

She builds a hut and then begins making weapons, something her people prohibited women to do. She succeeds in killing several dogs, but when the opportunity arises to kill their wounded leader, she cannot force herself to do it. Instead, she carries home his limp body and helps him to heal. It is as if she begins to realize that revenge should not drive her life, but survival should and that, as odd as it may seem, part of survival included compassion for others.

With the dog around, Karana notices her need for companionship and she realizes she had been very lonely without someone to talk to. Karana had a need to share feelings with others and for reciprocal relationships. Rontu becomes a loyal friend and leaves Karana only in old age to die in the lair that had once been home. During their time together on the island, Karana and Rontu developed relationships with other animals as well. Through these intimacies with animals, Karana vows to never kill another one.

Although Karana created relationships with Rontu, several otters, birds, and other animals, the need for *human* companionship never ceased. Authenticity implies that caring is dependent upon dialogue with others and reciprocal recognition. This means there must be mutual understanding of feelings. Karana and the animals do care; however, the levels of understanding and dialogue are quite different. With animals, it is difficult to tell what intentions are and if a rub against the leg means, you are special to me because I like you, or you are special to me because you feed me and give me shelter.

Nonetheless, when a group of otter hunters came to the island, Karana, although she hid from the hunters, befriended a young girl traveling with them. Despite language and culture barriers, they developed a trusting friendship. But when the young girl left with the hunters, Karana acknowledged her loneliness again. Karana continued to have a fulfilling life; however, she understood that she missed her friend Tutok and her sister Ulape and at times imagined hearing their voices in the wind and waves. The following concept summarizes Karana's movement toward authenticity (Figure 6.10).

Karana is eventually rescued and takes her new dog, Rontu Aru, and several other animal companions with her. Before she leaves the island, she proves her desire for human relationships is as alive as it had been eighteen years ago. She makes a sign with blue and white clay on her face. It was the same sign that her sister made when she was rescued, that meant she was still unmarried.

Karana develops toward authenticity in several ways. Not killing Rontu is the beginning of her movement. Even though the dog had killed her brother, Karana realized revenge was not the answer and that she could not do what she personally did not feel was right. She hunted in the past for revenge, for nourishment, and for sport. However, during her relationships with Rontu and other animals, she changed. Although she knew her family would ridicule her, she began to respect animals as if they were human.

The element Karana lacks in achieving authenticity is dialogue and reciprocal recognition, which the personified characters in *Charlotte's Web* demonstrate. Although she does have a short-term relationship with the Aleut

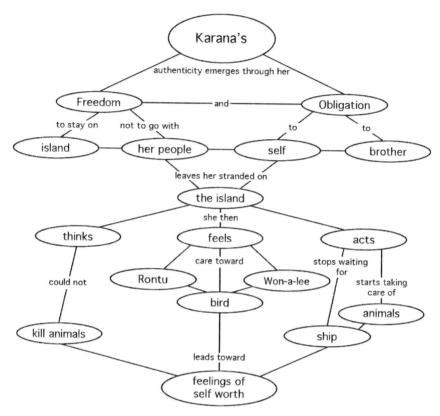

Figure 6.10. Concept map for *Island of the Blue Dolphins.*

girl, Tutok, when it is over, Karana has a more empty feeling than before. Perhaps Karana's willingness to leave the island to be with her people, instead of staying with the animals, portrays her need for reciprocity and potential relationships with others. It is, nonetheless, what she hopes to achieve. It is what makes us human, to have others in our lives with whom we can share intimacy and understanding: authentic reciprocity.

It is a human characteristic to be capable of developing intimate, caring relationships with other people. However, for relationships to flourish in classrooms, school needs to be a place where caring relationships are an essential element (Greene 1988). Every classroom has teachers trying to prepare children to live ethically in a democratic society. The whole language classroom seems to offer an excellent place for quality literature to be used to educate toward authenticity.

Project 2: High School
Improving High School Chemistry: Concept Maps and Vee
Diagrams
Hugh C. Pryor
Chemistry teacher
Flagler High School

Abstract

This article describes use of concept maps and Vee diagrams as instructional tools for high school chemistry. Concept mapping requires learners to draw relationships among concepts in a meaningful network. Vee diagrams help students understand the structure and process of knowledge construction. Compared to a traditional curriculum approach, these heuristics facilitated higher achievement. The usefulness of these heuristics to meet the recommended standards of teaching and learning in science and across the curriculum is emphasized.

Science education has been a topic of concern for many years. In their book *Best Practice*, Zemelman, Daniels and Hyde (1993) describe current standards for instructional excellence in: reading, writing, mathematics, science, and social studies. Drawing on recent reports from leading professional societies and research centers, they suggest: (a) less lecturing, (b) less student passivity, (c) less "covering" large amounts of material, (d) less rote memorization, (e) more emphasis on higher-order thinking, (f) more concentration on key concepts and principles, (g) deeper study of less topics, (h) more responsibility transferred to students, and (i) more collaborative activities.

Two heuristics: concept mapping and Vee diagramming may help to move high school chemistry teaching toward these goals. Both help students subsume new concepts into existing cognitive structures, and improve recall and test scores (Novak, 1990, 1991, 1993; Okebukola, 1992; Schmid and Telaro, 1990). Concept mapping requires learners to plot relationships among concepts in a meaningful organizational network within a specific knowledge domain (Novak, 1990; Okebukola 1992; Schmid and Telaro 1990). This strategy is based on Ausubel's assimilation theory (Ausubel and Novak 1978) that claims learning is influenced most by what the learner already knows. Concept mapping is effective in many disciplines: Literature (Leahy 1989), Biology (Novak 1990, 1993; Okebukola 1992; Schmid and Telaro 1990), Physics (Ross and Munby 1991; Roth and Roychoudhury 1993b), Earth Science (Ault 1985), Junior High School Science (Novak, Gowin and Johansen 1983) and College Chemistry (Zoller 1990; Cullen 1990). However, little is written about High School Chemistry to show how these heuristics may help

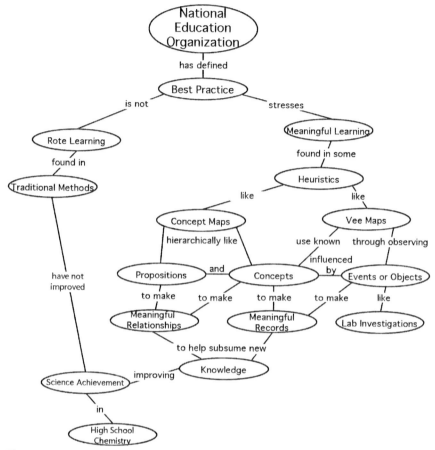

Figure 6.11. Concept map about improving high school chemistry.

to achieve aims described in *Best Practice*. Figure 6.11 shows the concept map that guided this study.

Figure 6.12 illustrates the Vee diagram guiding this study.

Students Taking Charge of Their Own Learning

Teacher-made maps can be used as master maps for evaluation of student-made maps and as examples and guides. However, as Schmid and Telaro (1990) indicate, total reliance on teacher-generated maps may result in rote learning. Novak and Gowin (1984) suggest that memorizing concept maps generated by others is rote learning, the opposite of what concept map construction encourages. Student-generated maps are the most important aspect

Research Question: Does the use of Concept Maps and Vee Diagrams improve achievement in High School Chemistry?

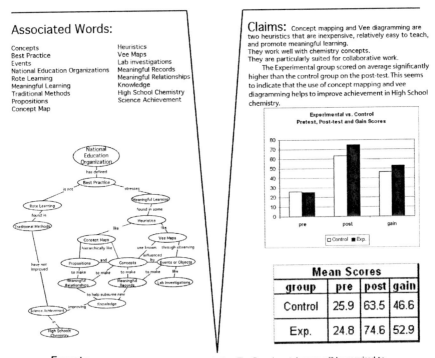

Associated Words:

Concepts
Best Practice
Events
National Education Organizations
Rote Learning
Meaningful Learning
Traditional Methods
Propositions
Concept Map

Heuristics
Vee Maps
Lab investigations
Meaningful Records
Meaningful Relationships
Knowledge
High School Chemistry
Science Achievement

Claims: Concept mapping and Vee diagramming are two heuristics that are inexpensive, relatively easy to teach, and promote meaningful learning.
They work well with chemistry concepts.
They are particularly suited for collaborative work.
   The Experimental group scored on average significantly higher than the control group on the post-test. This seems to indicate that the use of concept mapping and vee diagramming helps to improve achievement in High School chemistry.

Mean Scores			
group	pre	post	gain
Control	25.9	63.5	46.6
Exp.	24.8	74.6	52.9

Event: Use a 2 group, pretest, post test design. The Experimental group will be required to use and construct Concept maps and Vee Diagrams. The control group will not use the heuristics. Scores on the tests will be compared

Figure 6.12. Vee guiding the study about improving high school chemistry.

of concept mapping. Schmid and Telaro (1990) concluded that the process of creating a concept map was more important than the resulting map itself. This active learning achieves recommendations by Zemelman, Daniels and Hyde (1993) that students take charge of their own learning, are less passive, engage in higher-order thinking, and deeper study of a topic. The science teacher's role is as facilitator relying on judicious use of lecture, enhanced collaboration, and authority that helps promote student learning.

Real-world scientists frequently work in groups. Since learning science should be modeled after the process of science inquiry (Zemelman, Daniels and Hyde 1993), the use of collaborative groups makes pedagogical sense. Novak and Gowin (1984) suggest that when the construction of concept maps and Vee diagrams is done in small groups, they lead to classroom discussions, help negotiate meaning, and help correct misconceptions. Cooperative learning groups give the heuristics added strength and value (Novak 1981; Ault 1985; Schmid and Telaro 1990; Roth 1990; Okebukola 1992; Roth 1992; Roth and Roychoudhury 1993a; Roth and Roychoudhury, 1993b).

A short summary of this study will explain the value of concept mapping and Vee diagrams in high school chemistry. Classes were taught in 85 minute periods, 5 days a week for 4 weeks. The curriculum was based on materials from *Modern Chemistry* (Tzimopoulos, Metcalfe, Williams and Castka 1990). The unit was titled *Atoms: The Building Blocks of Matter*, covering atomic theory, the mole concept, percent composition, empirical and molecular formulas, Dalton's Atomic Theory, indirect observation, scientific method, isotopes, and percent composition of formulas. Each day, both groups received between 30-60 minutes of traditional instruction followed with supplemental materials. Both groups completed appropriate materials such as handouts, dittos, text questions, reports, etc. However, only students in the experimental group constructed concept maps about curriculum material, individually and in small groups. The control group was given supplemental material. Several labs were undertaken during the unit. The experimental group was required to collaboratively construct Vee diagrams about the laboratory experiment, the control group completed traditional lab reports.

The results of the pre-test and post-test administered to the 64 students indicated that concept mapping and Vee diagramming increased student test scores. There was a significant difference of eleven points between the two group's mean post-test scores, as shown in the Vee diagram that drove this study (Figure 6.12).

To test the difference in each group's ability to answer low and upper level questions each test question was judged according to criteria in Bloom's Taxonomy (Slavin 1988). The experimental group missed fewer lower level questions, indicating that Vee diagramming and concept mapping may offer methods to achieve pedagogical improvement in high school chemistry.

This study has practical implications for teachers. The answer to the focus question about usefulness of these heuristics in high school chemistry is: Yes! As tools, they are relatively easy to teach and inexpensive: treasured qualities in pedagogy.

Students using the heuristics seemed to make better connections among concepts. The results of this study are consistent with claims that these heuristics facilitate conceptual organization and serve as bridges for subsumption of new information (Okebukola 1992). In creation of Vee diagrams, students were compelled to think about: (a) how concepts fit together in an investigation, (b) what data to collect, (c) how best to interpret the data, and (d) how new information fit into previous knowledge.

Are these heuristics better than other techniques? They may be. This study suggests they improve achievement. Not only were scores higher for students using the heuristics, but there was significant difference in knowledge, comprehension, and application, and most importantly, problem solving skills.

Samples of Student Work

The four week study produced numerous concept maps and Vee diagrams. Figure 6.13 is a student concept map.

Figure 6.14 is an example of a Vee diagram completed by the same group two weeks after the unit was completed. Clearly as students gain practice in the use of concept mapping and Vee diagramming, they become better users of the heuristics.

Figure 6.13. Concept map by high school chemistry students.

Focus Question: How do the solubilities of the salts of group 2A vary?

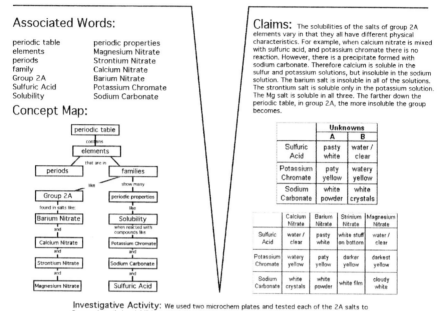

Associated Words:

periodic table	periodic properties
elements	Magnesium Nitrate
periods	Strontium Nitrate
family	Calcium Nitrate
Group 2A	Barium Nitrate
Sulfuric Acid	Potassium Chromate
Solubility	Sodium Carbonate

Concept Map:

Claims: The solubilities of the salts of group 2A elements vary in that they all have different physical characteristics. For example, when calcium nitrate is mixed with sulfuric acid, and potassium chromate there is no reaction. However, there is a precipitate formed with sodium carbonate. Therefore calcium is soluble in the sulfur and potassium solutions, but insoluble in the sodium solution. The barium salt is insoluble in all of the solutions. The strontium salt is soluble only in the potassium solution. The Mg salt is soluble in all three. The farther down the periodic table, in group 2A, the more insoluble the group becomes.

	Unknowns	
	A	**B**
Sulfuric Acid	pasty white	water / clear
Potassium Chromate	paty yellow	watery yellow
Sodium Carbonate	white powder	white crystals

	Calcium Nitrate	Barium Nitrate	Strinium Nitrate	Magnesium Nitrate
Sulfuric Acid	water / clear	pasty white	white stuff on bottom	water / clear
Potassium Chromate	watery yellow	paty yellow	darker yellow	darkest yellow
Sodium Carbonate	white crystals	white powder	white film	cloudy white

Investigative Activity: We used two microchem plates and tested each of the 2A salts to discover how their solubilities varied. We observed what happened to each salt when it was mixed with (a) potassium chromate, (b) Sodium Carbonate, and (c) Sulfuric acid. We recorded our data and used that data to find the identity of 2 unknown salts.

Figure 6.14. Vee by high school chemistry students.

Project 3: College Music
Introducing World Music Using Concept Maps
Deborah Jussela

Introducing World Music Using Concept Maps

Have you ever considered that ear training could be enhanced by listening with one's eyes? Concept mapping can help integrate hearing with seeing to improve learning about music. This was the aim in a World Music course taught at an introductory college level to non-music majors. Four key musical elements of rhythm, melody, form, and timbre were considered, and eight areas: Sub-Saharan African, Indian, Indonesian, Latin American, Eastern European, African American, Native American, and Japanese were explored. These areas were chosen from *Worlds of Music* by Jeff Titon (1996), which is an excellent introductory text accompanied by listening examples.

Concept mapping (Novak and Gowin 1984) was used to guide students through key concepts related to musical and cultural elements. A concept map is a learning tool that shows the relationships among key concepts in a network of meaning; maps are constructed in hierarchical order, with the most general concept at the top and related concepts below. After a semester of musical experience (3 hours per week for 15 weeks) that included listening, singing, dancing, drumming, and presentations, students emerged with a better understanding of world music cultures and themselves.

World Music

Although this course was taught at the college level, World Music is a humanities course that can be enjoyed by everyone. Units can be taught in elementary school as part of an interdisciplinary approach. At the middle school, World Music units are successful in rotational classes or wheel programs. Also, World Music can be offered as a semester class in high school, college, or community programs.

At the beginning of this course, a pretest of one minute music excerpts from several cultures was given. It was evident that most students were unable to identify them. Therefore, the challenge for teachers is to help students understand what music they are listening to, in order to analyze seemingly chaotic sounds into recognizable musical elements. This organized procedure for musical identification takes several steps and is an immersion learning process. The results were that by the end of the course, students were able to construct concept maps of the eight world music areas, and related cultural elements to show that they acquired a conceptual framework to evaluate their knowledge. This is one of the major benefits to using concept maps.

World Music Course Objectives

Multicultural Objectives

• heighten student's awareness of cultural identity and class member's cultural identity
• heighten understanding of cultures inside and outside community

Procedures and Activities

• concept map cultural and musical elements
• cooperative learning; small and large group discussion
• demonstrations and small group presentations
• hands-on drumming, singing, dancing
• viewing videos and films
• analysis of World Music on CDs, tapes, and records

Concept map uses

- personal cultural elements
- small group, large group or class
- world music cultural areas

Results

- defining musical and cultural elements
- breakdown of stereotypes and prejudices
- clarifies thinking

The World Music course outline was introduced using Figure 6.15. Three units covered by the teacher were: Africa, India, and Indonesia, and musical elements of rhythm, melody, form, and timbre. Rhythm is defined in *Webster's Dictionary* as "movement or fluctuation marked by the regular recurrence or natural flow of related elements" (1988, 1013). Melody is "a rhythmic succession of single tones organized as an aesthetic whole" (740). Form "suggests reference to both internal structure and external outline and often the principle that gives unity to the whole" (485). Timbre is "the quality of tone distinctive of a particular singing voice or musical instrument" (1235).

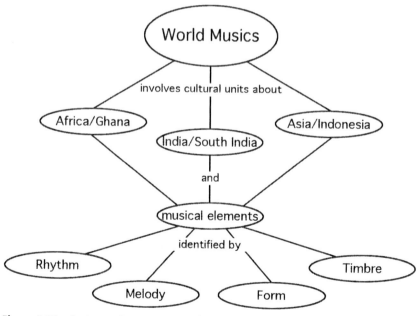

Figure 6.15.   Instructor's concept map for world music course.

Student presentations were about the music-cultures of Eastern Europeans, Native Americans, African Americans, Latin Americans, and the Japanese. For example, the Latin American presentation included elements in music from Ecuador.

To show how music fits into the broader culture, additional maps were constructed. Figure 6.16 shows the African unit's cultural and musical elements that the teacher presented. Music now becomes one of many cultural elements that students learned about and included in their cooperative group presentations. Culture, defined as "the customary beliefs, social forms, and material traits of a . . . social group" (314), includes: art, religion, language, sports, education, food, etc. Each presentation included at least six cultural elements in addition to music.

Students made a concept map for the culture they selected to present. After the small groups complete their concept maps, the teacher is able to determine if students understand the presentation format, the musical elements to be

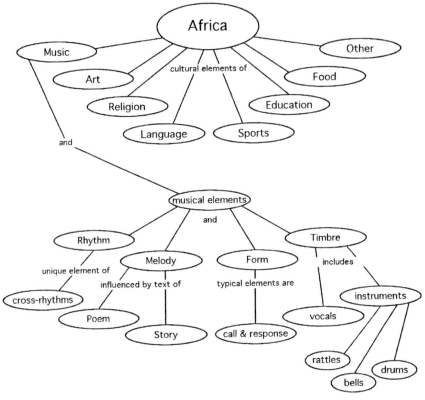

Figure 6.16.   Concept map about cultural elements of music.

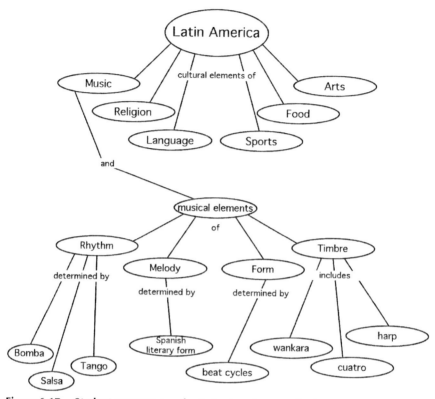

Figure 6.17. Student concept map for Latin American music elements.

identified, the seven cultural elements, and other pertinent information. The concept map helps the group to organize their thoughts, make decisions and choices, and can be reworked until the students agree on the concepts to be presented. The teacher can then meet with the groups to discuss and evaluate the concept maps.

Student Samples

Teachers can use concept maps to enhance understanding and clarify main ideas about World Music. Also maps can be used to introduce the course, a new unit, presentation guidelines, chapter reviews, testing, listening identification, and cultural elements. Student uses include: review for test preparation, presentation guideline organizer, listening identification and listening logs, portfolio entries, and small group presentations (Figures 6.17 and 6.18).

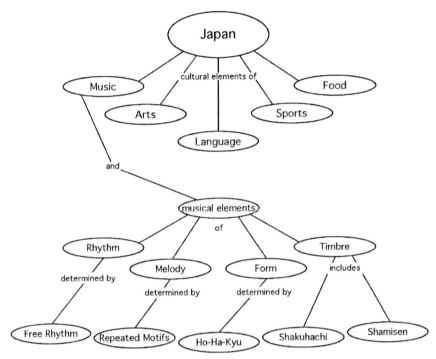

Figure 6.18.   Student concept map for Japanese music elements.

World Music Course

The first week began with an identification process of the students' own culture. This was done through concept mapping and discussion of individual, small, and large group cultural traits. Discussion focused on varied interpretations and meanings of concepts like culture and ethnomusicology. Each group made a concept map of their group elements to share with the class. Sample maps were discussed from the chalkboard or drawn on overhead transparencies to identify cultural traits. According to E.D. Hirsch (1988), knowledge in common shared by people creates characteristics of a national culture. Discussions aimed toward common knowledge to determine a class culture proved fruitful. This exercise helped students to identify cultural terminology and shared cultural elements.

An integral part of this course was hands-on musical performance of instruments, musical listening, musical analysis, and presentations. Students learned to play instruments of the three major areas presented by the instructor. Ensemble song rehearsals took place in class on a daily basis. At the end of each unit, students were able to identify and perform on each instrument in the World Music area.

Students kept a listening journal of selected musical recordings, analyzing over sixty pieces of music during the semester. Musical selections aligned with the cultural area of the readings and performance. The listening log helped students to analyze and identify musical elements and increased their ear training. After repeated listening, students were able to differentiate among various pieces of music.

The student class presentations were one hour long and covered the cultural elements selected by the group. Each group had a month to do research. Suggested research included personal interviews of community members, attendance at local multicultural festivals, visits to museums, libraries, multicultural internet sites, and world music concerts. Students were encouraged to create a genuine simulation or environment during their presentation. For example, the Native American presentation consisted of activities such as teaching of authentic powwow dances, sharing of food, wearing traditional leather clothing, sharing of artifacts such as bows and tools, reciting life stories, playing drums and rattles, and making a class totem pole. If authentic clothing could not be found, often students made representational outfits. In one case, a student made a Native American rattle from a turtle shell that he found while on a walk around the lake. The goal is to transform the classroom into that world music area for an hour, giving students an immersion experience into a particular culture.

By the end of the course, these non-music major students collectively decided to do a World Music performance for the public, giving back to the community some of what they learned. Because of these performances and workshops, multicultural knowledge is spreading and growing throughout our community. To date, students have performed in the World Music Ensembles for Volusia and Seminole County public schools, Stetson University's Multicultural Education Institute, The American Association of University Women, and Central Florida community groups.

FINAL THOUGHTS ABOUT PANELS, PAPERS, PRESENTATIONS AND PROJECTS

Authentic educating emphasizes personal meaning and responsibility and uses democratic principles to help students to reconstruct their experience. As I mentioned in the beginning of this book, authentic educating is project oriented, including personal and academic products, and I have given examples of each. With regard to the criteria of excellence regarding teaching, learning, curriculum and governance, I suggest these practical methods to involve students in active and meaningful learning, such as producing one-act plays, participating in panel discussions, or developing significant projects for the classroom, or personal journals to assess their own lives. I hope various suggestions summarized in this book show why it is important for educating to teach students how to learn and to enhance their growth toward authenticity.

This chapter shows that undergraduate and graduate students can use the heuristics of concept mapping and Vee diagramming effectively in analyzing sophisticated reading materials in order to present in a panel format. The heuristics help them focus their arguments and prepare them to respond to questions from an audience comprised of fellow students. It is important that students learn how to read and analyze material, but it is also important that they learn how to present information efficiently and coherently. Authentic educating entails students taking responsibility for their learning, but it is important that they can share their learning with others if they plan to become teachers.

The projects by Amy, Chris and Deborah show that undergraduates and graduate students can teach their students how to use concept maps and Vees to make student learning more effective and enjoyable. A key to authentic educating is that students are actively engaged in learning and, therefore, are able to use their learning to help others to learn.

Chapter Seven

The Future of Authentic Educating

I am optimistic about the future of authentic educating. I met a former student yesterday in the pottery studio at Stetson. I was trimming a vase I made the previous day on the potter's wheel as she said, "Getting in front of the class to talk about my journal and concept map made me realize that I no longer wanted to be a music major."

"You mean when you spoke in front of the class you felt detached from what you were planning?"

"Yes, exactly. I realized that being a music major didn't matter to me anymore. But it was having to concept map my life and write a journal that convinced me I had to change my major. If I didn't do that in your class I would never have realized it."

Since we were on Spring Break, I didn't expect to see any students, but life is like that, when one least expects to hear the answer one wants, one hears it. She played various roles in the play about several Aesop fables that she and a group of students from the music school produced. Her personal concept map was about choosing a music education career or going into art. As I looked up from the wheel, I said "I've been working on my book about authentic educating all day. Your comment convinces me that I am on the right track. Thanks. You sound excited about making the change. I wish you luck."

"Really, your class changed my life!" she responded, enthusiastically.

And so, how can I not be optimistic about authentic educating, especially, since I wrote in the first chapter that as teachers we change the world one person at a time. This chance encounter reminded me that teachers transform lives. And, authentic educating transforms them in ways that students realize that educating is not simply about curriculum, but the meaning of their lives.

Plato was suspicious of poets in *The Republic* (Cornford 1945). He even suspected the great Homer because the blind poet did not speak only of virtues, but of vices also. Plato spoke of an ideal world. So did Immanuel Kant. I gravitate more toward philosophers and poets who speak of the senses, of hearts and minds, who believe that humans are imperfect. When I think about authenticity, the words of Marianne Moore seem to capture its importance in her poem *Poetry* (Ellman 1976, 552) below.

Moore is artful in her assessment of the strengths and weaknesses of poetry. She is not interested in a "high sounding interpretation" but that poetry should be "useful." She is an advocate for the "genuine" and claims emphatically that, "we do not admire what we cannot understand." As a poet, she is not claiming certainty in the tradition of philosophers like Plato. She is a pragmatist. All she wants is that "if you demand on the one hand, the raw material of poetry in all its rawness and that which is on the other hand genuine, you are interested in poetry." This is the challenge that the poets present us with, to learn to blend thinking and feeling, to see what is genuine in the world and in ourselves, and poetry is a way.

POETRY

I, too, dislike it there are things that are important beyond all this fiddle.
Reading it, however, with a perfect contempt for it, one discovers in
it after all, a place for the genuine.
Hands that can grasp, eyes
that can dilate, hair that can rise
if it must, these things are important not because a

high-sounding interpretation can be put upon them but because they are
useful. When they become so derivative as to become unintelligible,
the same thing may be said for all of us, that we
do not admire what
we cannot understand: the bat
holding on upside down or in quest of something to

eat, elephants pushing, a wild horse taking a roll, a tireless wolf under
a tree, the immovable critic twitching his skin like a horse that feels a
flea,
the baseball fan, the statistician –
nor is it valid
to discriminate against "business documents and
school-books", all these phenomena are important. One must make a distinction
however, when dragged into prominence by half poets, the result is not poetry.

Another poet who would worry Plato is Archie Ammons (Ellman 1976, 892-5). His outstanding poem *Corson's Inlet* captures elements of authenticity. His sensual account of a walk along the dunes facing the sea in the "muggy sunny" morning sketches the poet's worldview as he contemplates the world surrounding him. Further on Ammons contemplates the particulars and the grand design.

CORSON'S INLET

I allow myself eddies of meaning:
yield to a direction of significance
running
like a stream through the geography of my work:
    you can find
in my sayings
        swerves of action
        like the inlet's cutting edge:
      there are dunes of motion,
organizations of grass, white sandy paths of remembrance
in the overall wandering of mirroring mind:

but Overall is beyond me: is the sum of these events
I cannot draw, the ledger I cannot keep, the accounting
beyond the account.

Ammons is an impressive observer of nature. But he is not a naturalist; he is a poet. And in conversations I had with him as a graduate student at Cornell, he impressed me with his talent and humility. He notes the geography of Corson's Inlet and the geography of his own work. Sorting the particulars does not add up to a complete picture. For him, "Overall is beyond me . . . " He will not leap to a metaphysical view. He knows what is beyond his ability. His "mirroring mind" is accurate, powerful in observation, but to mirror is not to know.

This is an issue that the philosopher Richard Rorty analyzed in detail in his famous book *Philosophy and the Mirror of Nature* (1981) in which he argues that there is no philosopher's stone for truth. The philosopher is in no privileged position when it comes to truth. The philosopher is tied to language, and language is interpretive not infallible. His answer to the paradox is presented in a subsequent book *Contingency, Irony and Solidarity* (1989) in which he argues for a pragmatic approach to philosophy that encourages dialogue and solidarity with others, that acknowledges the limits of knowledge. For him, the truths of Plato no longer apply; there is no way to know for certain what is true. The poet Archie Ammons seems to agree in the next excerpt from "Corson's Inlet".

> I see narrow orders, limited tightness, but will
> not run to that easy victory:
>   still around the looser, wider forces work:
>   I will try
>   to fasten into order enlarging grasps of disorder, widening
> scope, but enjoying the freedom that
> Scope eludes my grasp, that there is no finality of vision,
> that I have perceived nothing completely,
>   that tomorrow a new walk is a new walk.

Once again, the poets speak of experience and reason. But experience that does not lead to final answers, there is always the courage to contemplate the incomplete. Since authentic educating suggests that, "tomorrow a new walk is a new walk" the poet confirms a philosophic perspective. The noted philosopher of education, Tom Green (1984), as he developed his ideas about the "conscience of craft" saw the usefulness of poets. He acknowledged the value and power of metaphor in philosophy, and so, Plato's *Republic* seems to require poets when contemporary philosophers consider the nature of metaphysics and epistemology.

Since, as I develop the concept of authenticity, I blend existentialism and pragmatism, I see meaning and usefulness as key components of authentic educating. The poet e.e. cummings sides with feeling versus syntax, then develops a relationship of kisses as a "better fate than wisdom" (1959, 35). The poet extols feeling and connection as he contemplates the importance of this relationship in his view of life and beyond. I appreciate the poet's reliance on feeling, but also the philosopher's affinity for thinking. I do not rely on either completely, but prefer a flourishing integration of thinking and feeling to drive authentic action. I am advocating education that helps people to understand both their thinking and feeling. Contemporary philosophers seem to acknowledge the limits of reason and are beginning to see the importance of language and especially using language in dialogue. I favor those who value both thinking and feeling.

> since feeling is first
> who pays any attention
> to the syntax of things
> will never wholly kiss you;
>
> wholly to be a fool
> while Spring is in the world

my blood approves,
and kisses are a better fate
than wisdom
lady I swear by all flowers. Don't cry
the best gesture of my brain is less than
your eyelids' flutter which says

we are for each other; then
laugh, leaning back in my arms
for life's not a paragraph

And death I think is no parenthesis

Here the poet acknowledges the power of feeling. To pay attention to the "syntax of things" is at the expense of feeling the complete experience. As a poet, e.e. cummings stresses feeling, and questions the power of reason when he says "the best gesture of my brain is less than your eyelids' flutter." It is this emphasis on feeling that worried Plato about poets in *The Republic*, a bias that has lasted for twenty-five hundred years. Alfred North Whitehead acknowledges this bias in his famous statement that "The safest general characterization of the European philosophical tradition is that it consists of a series of footnotes to Plato" (Kaplan 1992, 584). There remain heirs to Plato in contemporary philosophy, and that is as it should be, because people want certainty. Unfortunately, it is an evasive ideal. However, I believe one can be authentic whether one believes as Plato did that truth is absolute, or if one is inclined to a relativist position—the evidence is in one's actions.

Hopefully, the theory and practice of authentic educating that I summarized in this book fits your interests in educating. The future then depends upon what we as individual teachers do with our students. This book has come full circle. I started by telling you that I wanted to be a teacher. I mentioned the trip around Manhattan Island in third grade, over fifty years ago. Although the World Trade Towers came and went tragically, the Statue of Liberty and the United Nations remain. As a student, accompanied by one of my favorite teachers, I felt inspired seeing these symbols of authenticity. I believe educating should help students become people who can embody these symbols as authentic citizens of the world. And so, I end saying, I hope what I wrote is helpful in your teaching. I will continue to work on my philosophy of educating; I wish you luck with yours . . .

References

Aesop. 1998. *The Complete Fables*. New York: Penguin Books.

Angelou, M. 1993. *I Know Why The Caged Bird Sings*. New York: Bantam Books.

Ault, C.R. 1985. Concept mapping as a study strategy in earth science. *Journal of College Science Teaching*, 37(2), 38-44.

Ausubel, D. and Novak, J. 1978. *Educational Psychology: A Cognitive View* (2nd ed.). New York: Holt, Rinehart & Winston.

Ayer, A.J. and J. O'Grady. 1992. *A Dictionary of Philosophical Quotations*. Cambridge, MA: Blackwell Publishers

Baker, C. 1968. *Ernest Hemingway: A Life Story*. New York: Avon Books

Banks, J. 1992. Dimensions of Multicultural Education. *Kappa Delta Pi Record*, 29 (1), 12.

Belenky, M.F.; Clinchy, B.; Goldberger, N. and Tarule, J. 1986. *Women's Ways of Knowing*. New York: Basic Books.

Bloom, A. 1987. *The Closing of the American Mind*. New York: Simon & Schuster.

Bloom, B.S. 1956. *Taxonomy of Educational Objectives: The Classification of Educational Goals, Handbook I: Cognitive Domain*. NewYork: Mckay.

Caedmon Records. 1965. *Ernest Hemingway Reading*. New York: Caedmon.

Cahn, S. M. 1997. *Classic and Contemporary Readings in the Philosophy of Education*. New York: McGraw-Hill

Campbell, J. 1995. *Understanding John Dewey*. Chicago: Open Court.

Camus, A. 1942. *The Stranger*. New York: Vintage.

Camus, A. 1957. *L'Etranger*. Paris: Librairie Gallimard.

Camus, A. 1988. *The Stranger*. New York: Alfred A. Knopf.

Camus, A. 1955. *The Myth of Sisyphus*. New York: Vintage Books.

Camus, A. 1961. *Resistance, Rebellion, and Death*. New York: Knopf.

Camus, A. 1972. *The Plague*. New York: Vintage Books.

Chaffer, J. 1988. *Thinking Critically*. New York: Houghton Mifflin.

Chopin, K. 1981. *The Awakening*. New York: Bantam Books.

Colangelo, N. and Davis, G. 1998. *Handbook for Gifted Education.* Boston: Allyn & Bacon.

Cornford, F.M. 1945. *The Republic of Plato.* New York: Oxford University Press.

Cullen, J. 1990. Using concept maps in chemistry: An alternative view. *Journal of Research in Science Teaching*, 27(10), 1067-1068.

cummings, e.e. 1959. *100 Selected Poems.* New York: Grove Press, Inc.

Diamond, A. and Edwards, L.R., Eds. 1988. *The Authority of Experience: Essay in Feminist Criticism.* Amherst: University of Massachusetts Press

Dailey, P. 2002. A Comparison of the Educational Philosophies of Volusia County Teachers with the Length of Time Teaching. (Master's thesis: Stetson University).

Dewey, J. 1916. *Democracy and Education.* Toronto, Canada: Collier- Macmillan Canada Ltd.

Dewey, J. 1938. Experience & Education. Toronto, Canada: Collier- Macmillan Canada Ltd.

Dewey, J. 1909. *Moral Principles in Education.* Carbondale, IL: Arcturus Books.

Eggen, P. and Kauchak, D. 2004. *Educational Psychology: Windows on Classrooms* (6th ed.). Upper Saddle River, NJ: Pearson.

Ellman, R. 1976. *The New Oxford Book of American Verse.* New York: Oxford University Press.

Ferrara, A. 1993. *Modernity and Authenticity: A Study of the Social and Ethical Thought of Jean-Jacques Rousseau.* Albany: State University of New York Press.

Foerster, N. 1957. *American Poetry and Prose.* Boston: Houghton Mifflin.

Gilligan, C. 1982. *In a Different Voice.* Cambridge: Harvard University Press.

Giroux, H.A. 1991. *Postmodernism, Feminism, and Cultural Politics.* Albany: State University of New York Press.

Goodman, K.S., Bird, L.B. and Goodman, Y.M. (Eds.). *The Whole Language Catalog*, Santa Rosa, CA: American School Publishers.

Gowin, D.B. 1981. *Educating.* Ithaca: Cornell University Press.

Green, T. 1984. *The Formation of Conscience in an Age of Technology: The John Dewey Lecture 1984.* Syracuse: Syracuse University.

Greene, M. 1988. *The Dialectic of Freedom.* New York: Teachers College Press.

Griffis, D. 1998. A Study to Assess the Validity and Reliability of the "Educational Philosophy Inventory" and to Establish Norms for Students, Teachers, and Cooperative Extension Professionals. (Master's thesis: Stetson University).

Heidegger, M. 1962. *Being and Time.* New York: Harper & Row.

Heidegger, M. 1959. *An Introduction to Metaphysics.* New York: Anchor Books.

Hemingway, E. 1952. *The Old Man and the Sea.* New York: Scribner Paperback Fiction.

Honderich, T. (Ed.). 1995. *The Oxford Companion to Philosophy.* New York: Oxford University Press.

Hirsch, E.D. Jr. 1988. *Cultural Literacy* (2nd ed.). Boston: Houghton Mifflin.

Hurston, Z.N. 1990. *Their Eyes Were Watching God.* New York: Harper & Row, Publishers.

Kaplan, J. 1992. *Barlett's Familiar Quotations (16th ed.).* New York: Little, Brown and Company.

Katz, M.S.; Noddings, N. and Strike, K. A. 1999. *Justice and Caring: The Search for Common Ground in Education.* New York: Teachers College, Columbia University.

King, C. 2000. A Comparison of the Educational Philosophies of Students Enrolled in Teacher Education Courses with those of Florida State Legislators. (Master's Thesis: Stetson University).

Knight, G.R. 1998. *Issues & Alternatives in Educational Philosophy* (3rd ed.). Berrien Springs, MI: Andrews University Press.

Leahy, R. 1989. Concept mapping: Developing guides to literature. *College Teaching*, 37(2), 62-69.

Leahy, R. 1996. Encouraging reflective practitioners: Connecting classroom to fieldwork. *Journal of Research and Development in Education*, 29(2). p. 104-114.

Leahy, R. 1994. Authenticity: From philosophic concept to literary character. *Educational Theory*, 44(4), 447-461.

Mager, R.F. 1962. *Preparing Instructional Objectives.* Belmont, CA: Fearon Publishers.

Malcolm, N. 1971. *Problems of Mind: Descartes to Wittgenstein.* New York: Harper & Row.

Malcolm, N. 1984. *Ludwig Wittgenstein: A Memoir.* Oxford & New York: Oxford University Press.

Mayeroff, M. 1971. *On Caring.* New York: HarperPerennial.

Merriam-Webster. 1988. *Webster's Ninth New Collegiate Dictionary.* Springfield, MA: Merriam Company.

McMillan, T. 1992. *Waiting to Exhale.* New York: Pocket Books.

Morrison, G.S. 2000. *Teaching in America (2nd ed.).* Needham Heights, MA: Allyn & Bacon.

Noddings, N. 1984. *Caring: A Feminine Approach to Ethics and Moral Education.* Berkeley, CA: University of California Press.

Noll, J.W. 1999. *Taking Sides: Clashing Views on Controversial Educational Issues (10th ed.).* Guilford, CI: Dushkin/McGraw-Hill.

Novak, J.D., Gowin, D.B. and Johansen, G.T. 1983. The use of concept mapping and knowledge vee mapping with junior high school science students. *Science Education*, 67(5), 625-645.

Novak, J.D. and Gowin, D.B. 1984. *Learning How to Learn.* New York: Cambridge.

Novak, J.D. 1990. Concept mapping: A useful tool for science education. *Journal of Research in Science Teaching*, 27(10), 937-49.

Novak, J.D. 1991. Clarify with concept maps. *The Science Teacher*, 58(7), 45-49.

Novak, J.D. 1993. How do we learn our lesson?: Taking students through the process. *The Science Teacher*, 60(3), 50-55.

O'Dell, S. 1960. *Island of the Blue Dolphins.* New York: Bantam Doubleday Dell Books for Young Readers.

Okebukola, P.A. 1992. Concept mapping with a cooperative learning flavor. *The American Biology Teacher*, 54(4), 218-221.

Parkay, F.W. and Stanford, B.H. 1998. *Becoming a Teacher* (4th. ed.). Needham Heights, MA: Allyn & Bacon.

Pryor, H.C. 1995. Imprivng High School Chemistry: Concept Maps and Vee Diagrams. (Master's thesis: Stetson University).

Ravitch, D. 1992. A Culture in Common. *Educational Leadership*. Vol. 49:4.

Rawls, J. 2001. *Justice as Fairness*. Cambridge, MA: Harvard University Press.

Rawls, J. 1971. *A Theory of Justice*. Cambridge, MA: Harvard University Press.

Rawls, J. 1993. *Political Liberalism*. New York: Columbia University Press.

Ross, B. and Munby, H. 1991. Concept mapping and misconceptions: A study of high school students' understandings of acids and bases. *International Journal of Science Education*, 13(1), 11-23.

Roth, W. M. 1990. Map your way to a better lab. *The Science Teacher*, 57(4), 31-34.

Roth, W.M. 1992. Dynamic evaluation. *Science Scope*, 15(6), 37-40.

Roth, M.R. and Roychoudhury, A. 1993a. Maps for more meaningful learning. *Science Scope*, 16(4), 24-25.

Roth, M.R. and Roychoudhury, A. 1993b. The concept map as a tool for the collaborative construction of knowledge: A microanalysis of high school physics students. *Journal of Research in Science Teaching*, 30(5), 503-534.

Rorty, R. 1981. *Philosophy and the Mirror of Nature*. Princeton, NJ: Princeton University Press.

Rorty, R. 1989. *Contingency, Irony and Solidarity*. New York: Cambridge.

Rowling, J.K. 1997. *Harry Potter and the Sorcerer's Stone*. New York: Scholastic Inc.

Runes, D. 1959. *Picture History of Philosophy*. New York: Bramhall.

Saint-Exupery, A. 2000. *The Little Prince*. New York: Harcourt, Inc.

Seuss, Dr. 1990. *Oh, the Places You'll Go!* New York: Random House.

Shepard, O. 1961. *The Heart of Thoreau's Journals*. New York: Dover Publications.

Schmid, R.F., and Telaro, G. 1990. Concept mapping as an instructional strategy for high school biology. *Journal of Educational Research*, 84(2), 78-85.

Slavin, R.E. 1988. *Educational Psychology: Theory into Practice*. New Jersey: Prentice Hall.

Tan, A. 1989. *The Joy Luck Club*. New York: Ballentine Books.

Taylor, C. 1991. *The Ethics of Authenticity*. Cambridge: Harvard University

Taylor, C. 1992. *Multiculturalism and "The Politics of Recognition"* Princeton: Princeton University Press.

Taylor, T. 1969. *The Cay*. New York: Avon Books.

Titon, J.T. 1996. *Worlds of Music*. New York: Schirmer Books

Tolstoy, L. 1981. *The Death of Ivan Ilyich*. New York: Bantam Books.

Thoreau, H.D. 1993. *Walden*. New York: Barnes & Noble.

Tuana, N., 1992. *Women and the History of Philosophy*. New York: Paragon Press.

Twain, M. 1996. *The Adventures of Huckleberry Finn*. New York: Barnes & Noble.

Tzimopoulos, N.D., Metcalfe, H.C., Williams, J.E. and Castka, J.F. 1990. *Modern Chemistry*. Austin: Holt, Rinehart and Winston.

Wassermann, S. 2004. *This Teaching Life: How I Taught Myself to Teach*. New York: Teachers College Press.

Wassermann, S. 2000. *Serious Players in the Primary Classroom*. New York:Teachers College Press.

Wassermann, S. 1993. *Getting Down to Cases.* New York: Teachers College Press.

Welty, E. 1978. *The Optimist's Daughter.* New York: Vintage Books.

White, E.B. 1952. *Charlotte's Web.* New York: HarperCollins.

Williams, M. 1981. *The Velveteen Rabbit.* Philadelphia: Running Press.

Wittgenstein, L. 1953. *Philosophical Investigations.* New York: The Macmillan Company.

Wittgenstein, L. 1980. *Culture and Value,* (translated by Peter Winch). Basil Blackwell: Oxford.

Woolf, V. 1989. *A Room of One's Own.* New York: Harvest.

Zemelman, S., Daniels, H. and Hyde, A. 1993. *Best Practices: New Standards for Teaching and Learning in America's Schools.* Portsmouth, N.H.: Heinemann.

Zoller, U. 1990. Students' misunderstandings and misconceptions in college freshman chemistry. *Journal of Educational Research,* 27(10), 1053-1065.

Index

acting, vii, 7-9, 40-41, 72, 90, 100
Adler, Mortimer, 21, 25, 43-44
AESOP, 61-64, 68-69, 105-6, 112
Ammons, Archie R., 147-48
Angelou, Maya, 73, 95, 98, 100-102, 113
Aristotle, 11, 22, 24-25, 27, 31-32, 43
Ausubel, David P., 59, 66, 132
authentic educating, v-vi, 1-6, 9, 11-17, 22, 34, 35, 37, 53, 61-63, 67, 72, 76-77, 79, 81, 83, 87-88, 105-6, 109, 112-19, 123, 143-45, 148-49; concept map, 4; defined, 3-4, 6; key to, 2, 12, 34, 72, 87, 105-6, 118, 144; value of, 3, 63, 76; Vee, 14, 77. *See also* educating
authenticity, v-vi, 2-4, 6-9, 15, 39, 69, 144, 146-49; characters, 71-73, 83-84, 90-94, 96-98, 100-105, 127, 130-31; concept maps, 6-7, 67, 89, 106-7, 109-10, 117, 128-29; defined, vii, 5, 68; movement toward, 72, 80-81, 88, 117, 127; personal journal, 69, 88, 94, 105-10; plays, 81, 112, 116; reaction papers, 94, 97-98, 101, 103, 114; Vee diagrams, 81, 112
authenticity inventory, 110
axiology, 21, 24, 38

Baker, Carlos, 67
Banks, James A., 46
Baum, L. Frank, 113
behaviorism, 20, 30, 31
Belenky, Mary F., 6
Bloom, Allan, 21, 44
Bloom, Benjamin, 3, 20, 52-53, 121, 135

Cahn, Steve M., 27, 78
Camus, Albert, 13, 20, 38-39, 73, 90-91, 113
caring, 5, 9, 11-12, 14, 16, 22, 68, 91, 100-101, 105, 114, 116, 130-31
Carter, Vince, 71
Catt, Amy, 127
Colangelo, Nicholas, 61, 126
Chopin, Kate, 83, 92, 113
concept maps, v, 3, 5, 14, 23-26, 42, 49-56, 63-65, 69-73, 78, 80-81, 84, 88, 105, 112, 117-20, 127, 132, 135, 137, 141, 144-45; examples: elementary, 51, 54, 64, 68-70; high school, 136; undergraduate, 28, 31, 33, 39, 45, 47, 78, 80, 82-83, 94-95, 99, 101, 140-42; graduate, 85, 123; papers, 129, 131, 133, 139; personal, 106-7, 109-10; presentations, 120, 124-26. *See also* heuristics

conceptual, 5, 14-15, 42, 52, 74-77, 79,
    85, 121, 135, 138
Cummings, e.e., 148-49

Dailey, Patricia, 47-48, 63
democratic ideals, 35, 37
Dewey, John, 6, 9-14, 20, 24-27, 30,
    33-37, 40, 45, 63, 110
dialogue, vii, 5-7, 9, 48, 62, 98, 101,
    102, 114-16, 128, 130, 147-48
documents of freedom and obligation,
    8, 35

educating, v, 5, 10-11, 13, 15-17, 34,
    40-45, 48, 88, 110, 112, 149. *See
    also* authentic educating
educational philosophy, 3, 6, 19, 43, 49
educational philosophy inventory, 3, 14,
    17, 35, 47
Emerson, Ralph W., 10
epistemology, 21-25, 38, 148
essentialism, 14, 20-21, 27-28, 30, 47, 48
existentialism, 3, 11, 13-14, 17, 20, 25,
    38-39, 47, 62, 114, 148

feeling, v, vii, 7-9, 13, 15, 31-32, 35,
    40-42, 49, 68, 72, 83, 90-91, 97, 107,
    110, 128, 130-31, 146, 148, 149
felt significance, vi, 9, 15-16, 41
four commonplaces, 5, 21, 40-41, 77
freedom, 5-8, 35, 37, 40, 89, 90, 94,
    102, 111, 114, 148
Freud, Sigmund, 33-34

Gardner, Howard, 3, 63
Gilligan, Carol, 6, 11, 91
Giroux, Henry, 21, 46
Gowin, D. Bob, v-vi, 2-3, 5-6, 9-10,
    14-16, 35, 40-43, 50, 52-53, 56-59,
    61, 66, 74, 76-77, 84-85, 88, 110,
    117, 127, 132-34, 137
Green, Thomas, 148
Greene, Maxine, 20, 88, 91-93, 110, 131
Griffis, David, 47-48, 63
growth, vi, 3-6, 19-20, 35-37, 40, 63,
    104, 109-10, 112, 144, 157

habits, 7-8, 10, 35, 37, 40, 42, 89-90
habitual dispositions, 7-8, 40-41, 93
Heidegger, Martin, 2, 20, 22, 38-39
Hemingway, Ernest, 66-67, 69, 71, 73,
    83-84, 113
heuristics, v, 3, 5, 14, 35, 42, 50, 53,
    72, 76, 77, 79, 85-88, 123, 127, 132,
    135-36, 144. *See also* concept maps,
    Vee diagrams, learning Vee
Hirsch, Eric D., 20, 29-30, 142
Hurston, Zora N., 73, 95-98, 113
Hutchins, Robert M., 21, 23, 43-44

intimacy, vii, 5, 7, 9, 97 98, 101, 103-4,
    114, 116, 131

James, William, 10, 24-25
Journals, 5-6, 16, 49, 65-66, 69, 73, 88,
    97, 105-10, 112, 117, 143-45
Jussela, Deborah, 137

Kant, Immanuel, 24, 27, 146
Katz, Michael, S., 12
King, Carol, 47-48, 63
Kohlberg, Lawrence, 11, 91
Knight, George R., 21, 23-25, 27-29,
    31-32, 34, 44, 46, 57
knowledge claims, 11, 22, 24, 74-76,
    121

Leahy, Robert, v-vi, 3, 5, 12, 14, 16-17,
    114, 127, 132
learning, v-vi, 1, 4-6, 10, 15, 18-19, 21,
    29, 30, 32-34, 40-42, 52-53, 57-59,
    61, 63, 65-66, 69, 71-72, 74, 77, 80,
    84-86, 105, 108, 112, 123, 132-38
learning Vee, 3, 5, 15, 50, 69, 71-72,
    74, 117. *See also* Vee diagrams,
    heuristics
Locke, John, 27
logic, 21-22, 24

Mager, Robert F., 53
Malcolm, Norman, 2, 16
Mayeroff, Milton, 9, 11, 13-14, 16, 105
McMillan, Terry, 73, 95, 102-3, 113